PLANTING PLANS
FOR YOUR
HOW TO CREATE A VEGETABLE, HERB
AND FRUIT GARDEN IN EASY STAGES
KITCHEN GARDEN

PLANTING PLANS
FOR YOUR
HOW TO CREATE A VEGETABLE, HERB AND FRUIT GARDEN IN EASY STAGES
KITCHEN GARDEN

HOLLY FARRELL

SPRING HILL

To Kevin

Published by Spring Hill, an imprint of How To Books Ltd.
Spring Hill House, Spring Hill Road, Begbroke, Oxford OX5 1RX United Kingdom
Tel: (01865) 375794 • Fax: (01865) 379162 • info@howtobooks.co.uk www.howtobooks.co.uk

First published 2013

British Library Cataloguing in Publication Data
A catalogue record of this book is available from the British Library.

ISBN: 978 1 908974 02 0

Produced for How To Books by Deer Park Productions, Tavistock, Devon
Designed and typeset by Mousemat Design Ltd
Printed and bound by Graficas Cems, Villatuerta, Spain

NOTE: The material contained in this book is set out in good faith for general guidance and no liability can be accepted for loss or expense incurred as a result of relying in particular circumstances on statements made in the book. Laws and regulations are complex and liable to change, and readers should check the current position with relevant authorities before making personal arrangements.

This book is not intended as a medicinal reference book, but as a source of information. The reader is advised not to attempt self-treatment using any herbal remedies without consulting a qualified medicinal herbalist. Neither the author nor the publisher can be held responsible for any adverse reactions to the recipes, recommendations and instructions contained herein, and the use of any herb or derivative is entirely at the reader's own risk.

CONTENTS

8. The Modules: Cut flowers   113

9. The Modules: Plants for pollinators and predators   127

10. The Modules: Grow your own garden supplies   145

PREFACE

When I started gardening, I was frustrated by the fact that all the books had endless detail about the different varieties of fruit and veg I could grow, and endless lists of all the things that could go wrong with that fruit and veg, but very little on how to go about laying out my plot. I was also wanting to grow lots of different things, not just the staples: cut flowers, edible flowers and herbs too, and few books included all of these things. I'd been inspired by the kitchen gardens of the great country estates, and wanted to recreate their functional beauty, on a small scale, on my allotment. Now I've trained with the Royal Horticultural Society, and been gardening for many years, I've written the book I wanted to read and use when I started out.

Of course I wouldn't have got this book to print without the help, support and encouragement of many people along the way. Chief among them is my husband Kevin, who tolerated the trials of living with a first-time author with patience and a smile. I am incredibly grateful to him for this and so much more. Huge thanks are also due to Sue Moss for all her sterling work on the illustrations, and Mum for her encouragement and proof-reading. Thanks also to Richard Farrell for tech support and web design, and to Marcia Peacock for horticultural advice. Finally, thanks to Nikki Read and Giles Lewis for taking a chance on an unknown.

INTRODUCTION

All you need to get started growing your own food and cut flowers is here: combine the planting plans in this book to turn your garden or allotment into a beautiful and productive space. Other kitchen gardening books leave it up to you to decide what to grow where. If you haven't the time or the confidence to worry about that, then this book is for you. You can create your own modular kitchen garden step by step, like a piece of modular furniture.

The chapters take you through the process of creating your kitchen garden a step at a time. First, assess your space and decide what you want to grow. Then dig the beds for your modules, and follow the instructions for sowing seeds and planting. The module plans show how to lay out each one. Finally, maintain your modules with the advice on basic garden tasks in the General Maintenance chapter. A glossary covers all the terms that may not be familiar.

Planting Plans for your Kitchen Garden is intended for beginners of any age and with any type of garden. There are more than 35 planting plans for vegetables, fruit, herbs and cut flowers, and plants to attract wildlife. Whether you want to grow easy summer salads or Brussels sprouts for Christmas, there is a plan you can use.

Chapter 1
HOW TO USE THIS BOOK

There are two main sections: the modules, and the 'how to' bits, which contain all the general advice on growing vegetables, fruit, herbs and cut flowers.

The first step is planning – assessing your site and deciding what you want to grow. Then choose your modules. Chapter 3 has plans showing possible combinations of modules for different situations, such as a garden to provide vegetables through the seasons, or a garden supplying fruit, edible flowers and flavourings for the home baker.

Once you have dug your beds and are ready to plant, use the planting plans for each module you've chosen to guide you in planting up the bed, following both the general advice in Chapter 4 and the specific advice for that module.

Each module plan is at a scale of 1:10, i.e. 1 centimetre (cm) on the plan represents 10cm on the ground. All the modules are 1 metre (m) by 2m. Use the plans to determine how far apart to space your plants. Each plant on the plans is drawn with a black dot in its centre – this is the point at which you should plant it. Not all the plants can be shown on some plans, so check the table in the module detail for how many plants are needed.

The potential yields of the fruit and vegetable modules are given. These are the average harvests you can expect without major (pest or disease) problems from each module in a growing season. The average potential yields for the fruit modules are of mature plants – don't expect as much in the first couple of years.

Chapter 11 has all the advice on how to maintain your modules through the year. However, you won't find off-putting long lists and gruesome pictures of all the things that could go wrong. To sort a particular problem, see the Further Reading section for sources of advice.

How to garden
Growing plants is relatively straightforward, and growing your own food and flowers will fill you with pride and satisfaction. Plants have evolved and been bred to perform as well as they can, and all you really need to do is supply space for them to do their thing. Your kitchen garden will be bountiful and beautiful, but it will never be perfect. You will set yourself up for disappointment if you think that it's all going to be a bed of roses. Be realistic about the factors out of your control – you should be prepared to lose plants. One year you have tomatoes coming out of your ears. The next year you lose them all to disease, but your sweet peas do amazingly well. This is the swings and roundabouts nature of gardening – it is both wonderful and heart-breaking. So don't be disheartened, and definitely don't give up. Learn from your mistakes, enjoy your success, and start planning next year.

Chapter 2
YOUR GARDEN OR ALLOTMENT

ASSESSING THE AVAILABLE SPACE

Where do you live?

Although the UK's climate has recently been (and may continue to be) rather off-kilter, basic rules still apply. If you live in the north your sowing and planting-out times can be several weeks behind those of gardens in the south. You are also more likely to suffer late spring and early autumn frosts, so are more likely to need to protect your crops. Plan what you can grow accordingly, so for example crops that need a long season to mature will do less well.

You should also take the average rainfall for your area into account. If you live in the dry South East and want to grow crops that need a lot of water you may have to spend more time in the garden watering than if you live in the wetter North West.

On top of your garden or allotment's location, it will have its own microclimate – specific variations in sunlight, temperature and more that can create very different growing conditions to those in your neighbour's garden. Assessing these (see below) will give you an idea of what to expect when you start to create your kitchen garden.

How much sun does it get?

South-facing space is ideal: it gets the most sun from dawn to dusk, warming the soil and giving plants essential sunlight for photosynthesis. However, even north-facing gardens can successfully grow most crops by planting in the sunniest spots.

Watch how the sun tracks round your garden during the day – remember this will be different in the winter and the summer – and make a note of which areas are in the sun for longest. These are your ideal spots for locating module beds.

How sheltered is it?

Walls and fences can cast shade and create rain shadows (that bit at the bottom of the wall/fence that's always dry), but they are also useful. Brick walls in particular soak up the sun's heat during the day and release it slowly, so they are ideal to grow crops like tomatoes and peppers against.

Wind

Does the wind rush through your garden or eddy around it at the bottom of solid walls? Semi-permeable barriers such as hedges are better to shelter gardens from strong winds as they slow the wind down without creating turbulence on the other side. If you can, create your modules out of direct winds, and if you are in an exposed spot remember you are likely to have to stake most of your tall plants.

Frost pockets

Gardens and allotments at the bottom of valleys or slopes, especially where there is then a fence, wall or other barrier, can create frost pockets – areas where frost is quick to settle and slow to lift because the cold air that travels down the slope gets trapped by the barrier. Again, if you can, avoid siting your modules where you've noticed the frost stays on the grass much longer than anywhere else.

What's your soil like?

Good soil is the foundation of all good gardening, but you don't need perfect loam to have a successful garden. Plants grow all over the world in the most unlikely and difficult situations, and you can improve your soil considerably over the years. However, it's important to know what type of soil you have before you start so you know what will do best there and how to go about improving it.

Ideally you will have a loamy soil with a deep topsoil profile and plenty of organic matter and soil organisms (worms, insects, bacteria and fungi). Hardly any gardeners have this soil, and if they do they almost certainly didn't start off with it. You can go a long way towards creating good soil (in the long-term) by the continual addition of organic matter every year, and by not compacting or disturbing it unduly by walking/treading on it unnecessarily.

To find out what kind of soil you have, dig up small amounts from various places in your garden and mix them all together. Take a bit of the mixture, add a few drops of water and roll it into a ball in your hand. If if sticks together easily as you manipulate it, it tends towards the clay end of the scale. If it falls apart like sand it, unsurprisingly, tends towards the sandy end of the scale. You may also have elements of chalk or silt in your soil, characterised by white particles and a silky feel respectively. See page 41 for how to improve soils with a high proportion of clay or sand.

Soil pH

Certain soil types can have extreme pH levels, and it's useful to know if your garden's soil falls into this category as it can affect the growth of your plants. Thin, chalky soils over limestone can have a strongly alkaline pH, which is good for growing brassicas but not a lot else. Strongly acidic soils inhibit the presence of soil organisms, especially worms, which prevents the breakdown of organic matter and the release of essential nutrients.

Most garden centres sell rudimentary pH testing kits you can use for your soil, or you can pay to send off a soil sample to the Royal Horticultural Society (RHS) for testing (they will also assess your soil type and its nutrient content). As most plants grow best in roughly neutral pH soil (pH 6.5–7.5), this is what to aim for.

However, everything between pH 5.5 and pH 8 is fine, just keep adding organic matter every year. Add lime and alkaline organic matter (mushroom compost, well-rotted horse manure) to very acidic soils. Strongly alkaline soils are best improved by adding garden compost and just growing on it all the time. Sulphur chips can be used but can have the effect of breaking down more limestone which only raises the alkalinity again.

Bottom line

Plants want to grow, and while they may be temperamental in extreme soils or weather conditions, you are unlikely to have major disasters wherever you are growing your modules. Put them in the best spot you have and look after the soil and they will respond well.

BEETROOT
Boltardy
Top selling variety

CARROT
Resistant to carrot fly...
SOW: Mar-Jul
HARVEST:

Borage

tuce
llo Rossa'

RUNNER BEAN
Scarlet Emperor
Early cropping, traditional favourite

SOW: Apr-Jun
HARVEST: Jul-Oct

Rich in Vitamins & Minerals

For recipes, growing tips and more, visit

rhs.org.uk/thankyo

RHS GROW YO

RADISH
ed salads

Chapter 3
CHOOSING THE MODULES

WHAT DO YOU WANT TO GET OUT OF IT? DECIDING ON WHAT TO GROW

Now you know what you can grow in your garden, you can decide what you want to grow. You are likely at this stage to be chomping at the bit to be out there with your trug, picking beans and pulling up carrots, eating one strawberry for every two you put in the bowl and gathering armfuls of fresh flowers. Without wanting to rain hailstones on your horticultural heaven, BE REALISTIC! The number one cause of gardens and allotments being abandoned to a weedy jungle is over-ambition. The beauty of the modular system is that you don't have to do everything at once, you can put in one module at a time.

All the modules are designed to be small and relatively easy to maintain, but still, low-maintenance does not mean no maintenance. You will have to get out there to weed and water. If you're not sure how much time you'll have, don't put in six modules straight away, start with one or two and see how you go. Garden centres sell young vegetable plants as well as flower plants, so if you decide you want more by mid-summer, it's not too late.

The more experienced you become at gardening, the less time you will need to maintain your modules. Some modules will be more labour-intensive than others. In general, those with trees or shrubs will take the least looking after, the herbaceous perennials a little more time, and the annual modules the most. Allow half an hour a week per annual module, not including watering, but remember, 10 minutes a day is easier than hours at the weekend.

Now it is purely down to what you want to grow. Only grow what you know you want to eat. If you never buy courgettes in the shops, you're not going to eat them from the garden either. If you're always buying fresh herbs, then consider growing the herbs modules.

Consider your perennial/annual mix in terms of crop rotation (see p. 10) and, finally, decide if you have space for any pollinator/predator modules.

CREATING A DESIGN WITH YOUR CHOSEN MODULES

This part is entirely up to you. Use one of the suggested layouts of modules in the garden plans that follow, or create your own design. Your layout will fundamentally be dictated by what space you have and whether you want space for socialising, children's games, etc.

Remember that you will need a path at least 60cm wide between each bed. This is wide enough to weed from, but make some of your paths wider for a wheelbarrow (and lawnmower). If you are going to use permanent protective structures like fruit cages, take their dimensions into account as well.

You are more likely to use and maintain your modules regularly if you only have to pop out the back door to get to them, so don't shove them out of sight at the end of the garden. Put modules of things you use most often – herbs, salads – closest to the house.

Scaling the modules up or down

All the modules are a basic size of 1m by 2m, so most gardens will have room for at least one or two. The average vegetable and fruit yields are included, but roughly speaking they would each supply enough for two people.

However, if you want to grow more, for more people, or for preserving (e.g. as jam or ice cream), it is very easy to scale the modules up. You may instead want to grow only one half of a module, leaving out the crops in the other half to make a square bed – it's up to you.

Avoid making beds too wide. To avoid compacting the soil it's best not to walk on the beds whenever possible. The modules are 1m wide so that you can reach to the middle to harvest or weed without stepping on the soil. If you want to double the width, work off a plank to spread your weight.

Crop rotation

Crop rotation is not something to worry about unduly. There is a standard formula for vegetable plots, but in a modular garden you may not be growing every element from the formula, and the beds do not contain exclusively brassicas or beans, for example. The regular incorporation of organic matter, and maintaining a healthy, biodiverse garden, will go a long way towards combating the problems crop rotation is used to avoid.

In essence, you don't want to grow the same crop in the same place two years running. Vegetables and other annuals are hungry for nutrients, but as each crop has different nutritional requirements, the soil can be depleted for one type of vegetable but not for another. Rotation also prevents a build-up of specific pests and diseases in the soil.

If you are including two or more annual modules within your plan, work out a rotation. If you only have space for one annual bed, grow a different module in it every year, or at least rotate the planting by 180°. Keep a note or photo of what was where every year. Perennial beds, even those that have a mix of annuals and perennials, stay where they are once planted; the incorporation of organic matter will refresh the annual sections.

Garden Plan: a small kitchen garden

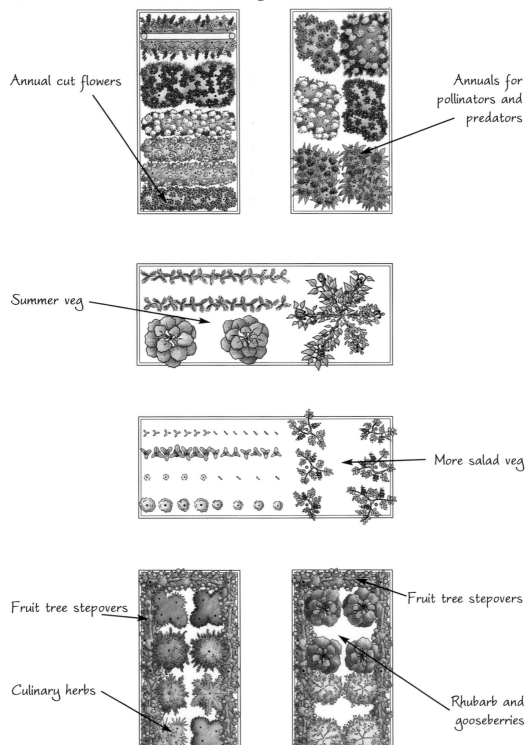

Annual cut flowers

Annuals for pollinators and predators

Summer veg

More salad veg

Fruit tree stepovers

Culinary herbs

Fruit tree stepovers

Rhubarb and gooseberries

Garden Plan: **A SMALL KITCHEN GARDEN**

Including all the main elements of a traditional kitchen garden – vegetables, herbs, fruit and cut flowers – this design also makes room for a pollinators bed. There are two perennial beds of herbs and soft fruit, both surrounded by stepover apples or pears, behind which four annual beds supply you with a good variety of summer vegetables and cut flowers, and annual flowers to attract pollinators and predators.

A small kitchen garden combination will give you a taste of growing your own food, with all of the produce focused in the summer months, when it's much easier to get motivated to go and do a bit of weeding. Longer-term commitment is only on the soft fruit and herbs beds. The fruit tree stepovers could be left until a later date if you are not sure.

Modules in this garden

Module name (and number)	Size	Page reference
Annual cut flowers (25)	2m x 1m	117
Annuals for pollinators and predators (30)	2m x 1m	131
Summer veg (3)	2.5m x 1m	59
More salad veg (2)	2.5m x 1m	57
Fruit tree stepovers (24)	2m x 1m	111
Culinary herbs (13)	2m x 1m	85
Rhubarb and gooseberries (21)	2m x 1m	105

Scaling up the modules
- For Module 2, extend the rows of lettuce and beetroot by 25cm each. This means you can station sow (p. 42) four lettuces per row, and just extend the drill for the beetroot.
- For Module 3, increase the length of the carrot rows by 50cm. Increase the spacing between the two courgette plants to 90cm and 30cm from either end of their section.

Garden plan: easy-to-grow kitchen produce

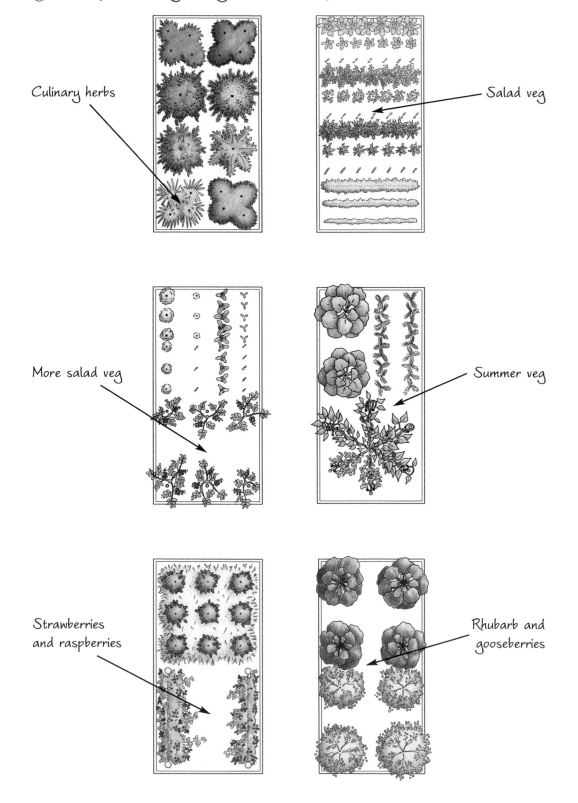

Culinary herbs

Salad veg

More salad veg

Summer veg

Strawberries
and raspberries

Rhubarb and
gooseberries

Garden Plan: **EASY-TO-GROW KITCHEN PRODUCE**

These modules have been combined to make a productive plot of crops that need no expertise to grow well. If you are not confident in your gardening abilities, you may consider this combination. The focus is summer vegetables – salads, beans, courgettes and more – all of which crop well with little encouragement, plus perennial fruit that more or less looks after itself. Add a bed of herbs and you've got a good selection of home-grown produce to use in the kitchen all summer.

Half of the modules are annual, half are perennial herbs and soft fruit. The perennial beds mean there is some longer-term commitment to the garden, but they are also lower maintenance once planted. If you have the space and time, consider adding a bed or two of pollinators and predators modules. None of the modules is changed in size from the standard layout given in the module plans, so there is no need for scaling up or down.

Modules in this garden

Module name (and number)	Size	Page reference
Culinary herbs (13)	2m x 1m	85
Salad veg (1)	2m x 1m	55
More salad veg (2)	2m x 1m	57
Summer veg (3)	2m x 1m	59
Strawberries and raspberries (18)	2m x 1m	99
Rhubarb and gooseberries (21)	2m x 1m	105

Garden plan: vegetables and herbs for the serious cook

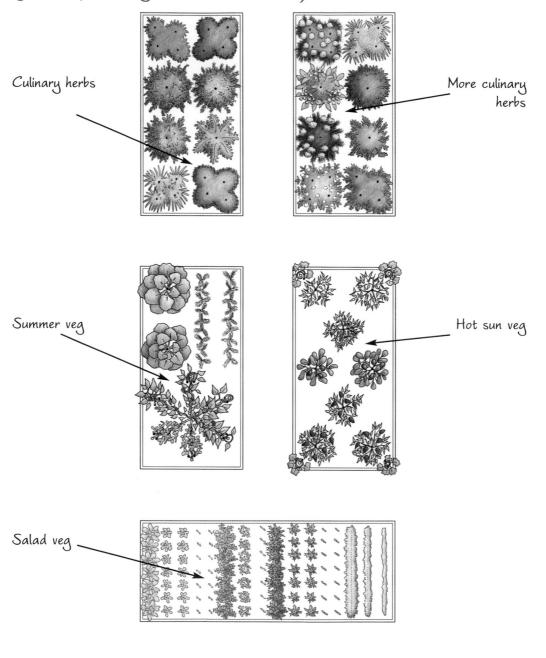

Culinary herbs

More culinary herbs

Summer veg

Hot sun veg

Salad veg

Spring and late summer veg

Garden Plan: **VEGETABLES AND HERBS FOR THE SERIOUS COOK**

These modules are a bit more adventurous. There is no fruit, as the focus is on herbs and vegetables that go beyond the basic ingredients to include produce that is harder to find really fresh in the shops. For example, you will really notice the difference in taste between a shop-bought broad bean and one freshly podded moments after being picked.

Modules in this garden

Module name (and number)	Size	Page reference
Culinary herbs (13)	2m x 1m	85
More culinary herbs (14)	2m x 1m	87
Summer veg (3)	2m x 1m	59
Hot sun veg (6)	2m x 1m	65
Salad veg (1)	2.5m x 1m	55
Spring and late summer veg (4)	2.5m x 1m	61

Scaling up the modules
- For Module 1, add an extra row of cut-and-come-again salad leaves and an extra row of rocket into your successional sowing.
- For Module 4, lengthen the rows in each half by 25cm, which means you can squeeze in another seed potato per row, another broad bean plant per row, and have longer drills of beetroot, fennel, pak choi and radicchio.

Garden plan: a family plot

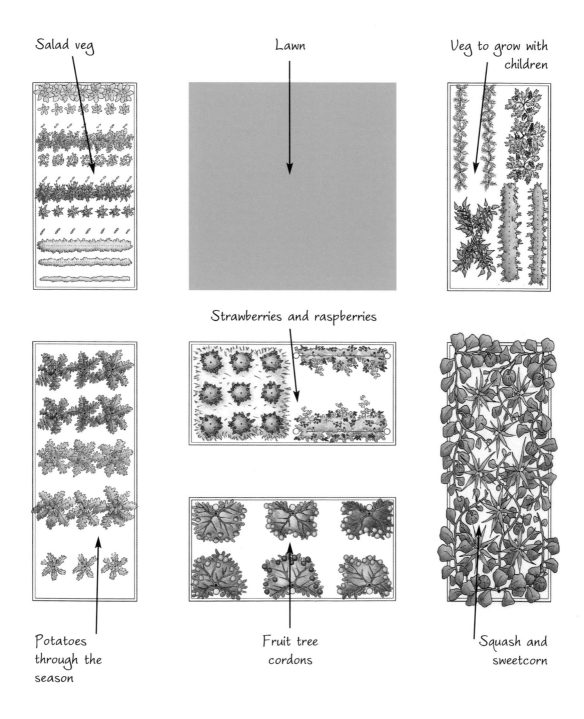

Salad veg

Lawn

Veg to grow with children

Strawberries and raspberries

Potatoes through the season

Fruit tree cordons

Squash and sweetcorn

Garden Plan: **A FAMILY PLOT**

The modules here are all chosen with children in mind: vegetables with quick returns, easy-to-grow fruit, veg that tastes so good straight from the plant no child will refuse it, the magic of planting one potato then digging up many more. There is also space for a lawn or patio area so the whole family can enjoy being outdoors and in the garden.

As a busy family will necessarily decrease the time you have to maintain a garden, the modules are mostly lower maintenance ones as well. The two fruit modules require only a little attention, and the potatoes and squash/sweetcorn modules once planted can also be left to grow away happily by themselves: both cover the ground nicely and should suppress weeds too. The highest-maintenance modules are placed nearest the house to make it easier to pop out to do 5 minutes' weeding when you have a chance.

Modules in this garden

Module name (and number)	Size	Page reference
Salad veg (1)	2m x 1m	55
Veg to grow with children (11)	2m x 1m	75
Potatoes through the season (9)	2.5m x 1m	71
Squash and sweetcorn (12)	2.5m x 1m	77
Strawberries and raspberries (18)	2m x 1m	99
Fruit tree cordons (23)	2m x 1m	109

Scaling up the modules
- For Module 9, add in another row of first early potatoes; add an extra 10cm of spacing between the salad potatoes and the maincrops and another 10cm between the maincrops and the edge. The spacings should then be as follows: 20cm – first earlies – 40cm – first earlies – 40cm – second earlies – 60cm – salad – 70cm – maincrop – 30cm.
- As the squash or pumpkins will happily expand to fit whatever space they are given, increase the length of Module 12 but don't alter the planting or spacings.

Garden plan: a shady garden

Winter stems and spring bulbs

Rhubarb and gooseberries

Early spring-flowering plants for pollinators

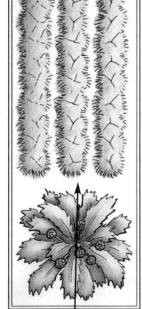

Permanent veg plants

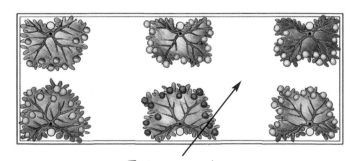

Fruit tree cordons

Garden Plan: **A SHADY GARDEN**

All is not lost if you have a shady garden – you can still grow vegetables, fruit and cut flowers. This combination has been designed for a garden with little direct sunlight.

Perennial plants will do better in a shady spot. Gooseberries and raspberries, plus fruit tree cordons of apples, pears or plums, will keep you well-supplied, and globe artichoke and asparagus will be a welcome addition to the kitchen. Some spring bulbs and winter stems will brighten up the garden and the home, and a half-module of pulmonaria and primroses will flourish in the shade and provide early nectar for bees.

Modules in this garden

Module name (and number)	Size	Page reference
Winter stems and spring bulbs (27)	2.5m x 1m	121
Rhubarb and gooseberries (21)	2.5m x 1m	105
Fruit tree cordons (23)	2.5m x 1m	109
Permanent veg plants (7)	2.5m x 1m	67
Early spring-flowering plants for pollinators (32)	1m x 1m	135

Scaling up the modules
- For Module 27, double the hellebores section.
- For Module 21, increase the spacing of the gooseberries to 1.05m between plants. Although there is not room to add another plant, the extra space will allow them to get bigger and bear heavier crops. Increase the spacing of the rhubarb to 1.05m as well, but here there is room to add another plant to create a pattern of the five dots on a die.
- In Module 23, increase the space between cordons to 1m. You could add two extra cordons in the middle, again creating a five-dots-on-a-die pattern in each half.
- For Module 7, an extra 50cm (three plants) can be added to the rows of asparagus, as there is not enough space to add another artichoke.
- The early-spring pollinators module is cut in half. A central pussy willow shrub is underplanted with six pulmonaria and six primrose plants.

Garden plan: veg through the year

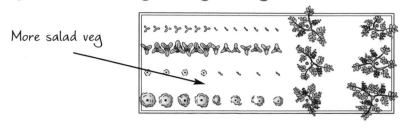

More salad veg

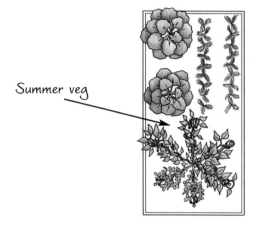

Summer veg

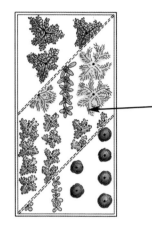

Spring and late summer veg

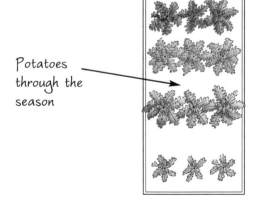

Potatoes through the season

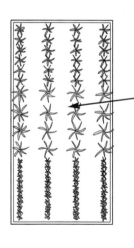

Onions and garlic

Winter veg

Garden Plan: **VEG THROUGH THE YEAR**

There's no doubt it is easier to go out and do some work in the garden when the sun is shining and the birds are singing than when it's cold and damp in the depths of winter. However, having food you have grown yourself all through the year, even if it's only small quantities, is extremely satisfying. This combination allows you to have home-grown parsnips and sprouts for your Christmas dinner, potatoes and broad beans in spring, a wealth of summer vegetables and stored onions and garlic all year round.

All these beds are annual beds, so rotating to grow next year's crops is easy. Modules can also be easily changed for another if you want to grow something different next year – pumpkins and squash store well. Make some room if you can to add in some pollinator/predator modules to benefit your crops and add some flower colour to your garden.

Modules in this garden

Module name (and number)	Size	Page reference
More salad veg (2)	2.5m x 1m	57
Summer veg (3)	2m x 1m	59
Spring and late summer veg (4)	2m x 1m	61
Potatoes through the season (9)	2m x 1m	71
Onions and garlic (5)	2m x 1m	63
Winter veg (8)	2.5m x 1m	69

Scaling up the modules
- For Module 2, extend the rows of lettuce and beetroot by 25cm each. This means you can station sow four lettuces per row, and just extend the drill for the beetroot.
- Extending Module 8 allows you to increase the length of the parsnip rows by 50cm, and add a fourth sprouts plant.

Garden plan: garden produce for bakers and jam-makers

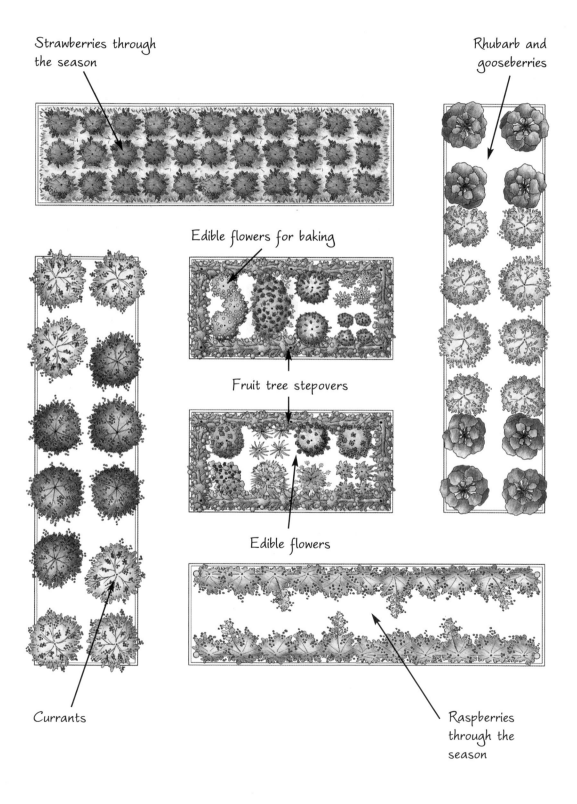

Strawberries through the season

Rhubarb and gooseberries

Edible flowers for baking

Fruit tree stepovers

Edible flowers

Currants

Raspberries through the season

Garden Plan: **GARDEN PRODUCE FOR BAKERS AND JAM-MAKERS**

This combination fits a lot of fruit into a small space, and also adds herbs and edible flowers for cake flavourings and decoration. All of the beds are entirely or mostly perennial, so need little attention other than keeping the weeds down and an annual prune. It may take a few years for the shrub fruit to reach a size where you can get enough fruit for a decent batch of jam, but even in the first year you could make enough to accompany your (home-grown) lavender scones.

If you are wanting to grow fruit to make jam with, choose strawberries and raspberries that all ripen around the same time, rather than through the season. It's a pretty garden, but unfortunately the birds will also find your red berries attractive, so you may want to invest in some netting or cages to keep them off while the fruit is ripening.

Modules in this garden

Module name (and number)	Size	Page reference
Strawberries through the season (18)	3.5m x 1m	101
Rhubarb and gooseberries (21)	4m x 1m	105
Raspberries through the season (20)	3.5m x 1m	103
Currants (22)	4m x 1m	107
Edible flowers for baking (17)	2m x 1m	93
Edible flowers (16)	2m x 1m	91
Fruit tree stepovers (24)	2m x 1m	111

Scaling up the modules
- Add another five rows of three plants to Module 18, making 33 plants overall.
- For Modules 21 and 22, simply double the bed, either putting all the same plants together or alternating them (putting all the same plants together will be easier for netting the fruit; the rhubarb will not need protecting from the birds).
- In Module 20, lengthen the rows, adding five plants to make 11 plants per row.

Garden plan: a mostly annual kitchen garden

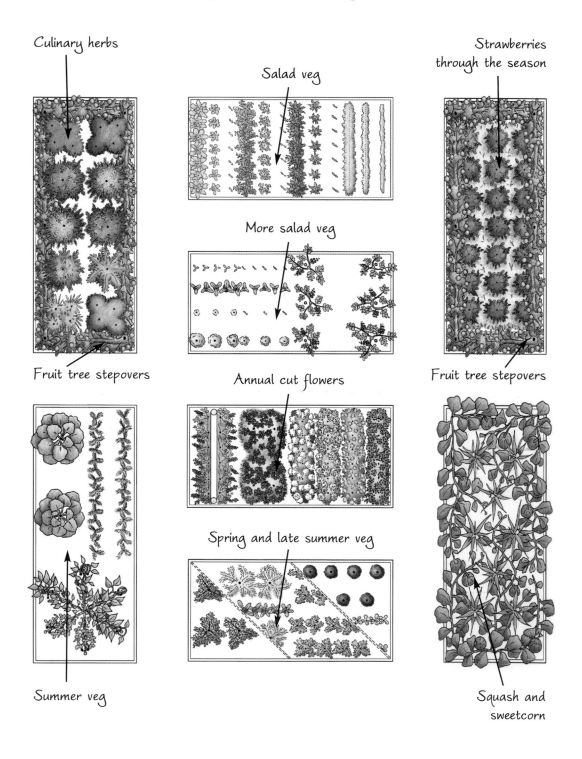

Culinary herbs

Salad veg

Strawberries through the season

Fruit tree stepovers

More salad veg

Fruit tree stepovers

Annual cut flowers

Summer veg

Spring and late summer veg

Squash and sweetcorn

Garden Plan: **A MOSTLY ANNUAL KITCHEN GARDEN**

This kitchen garden plan incorporates eight modules and therefore requires more space than some of the other gardens. Using six annual modules, it is a relatively cheap way to establish a kitchen garden of vegetables, fruit, herbs and cut flowers. The two perennial modules utilise their space as effectively as possible by overlaying fruit tree stepovers.

Modules in this garden

Module name (and number)	Size	Page reference
Culinary herbs (13)	2.5m x 1m	85
Strawberries through the season (19)	2.5m x 1m	101
Fruit tree stepovers (24)	2.5m x 1m	111
Salad veg (1)	2m x 1m	55
More salad veg (2)	2m x 1m	57
Summer veg (3)	2.5m x 1m	59
Squash and sweetcorn (12)	2.5m x 1m	77
Annual cut flowers (25)	2m x 1m	117
Spring and late summer veg (4)	2m x 1m	61

Scaling up the modules
- To increase the size of Module 13, plant two each of rosemary and oregano in the middle, planting them diagonally opposite each other to create a mini-chequerboard.
- Add a row of strawberries to Module 19.
- For Module 24, keep the number of trees the same and plant them in the same places, i.e. the corners and halfway up each side. The extra length allows you to grow each one a little longer, so they will bear more fruit.
- For Module 3, increase the length of the carrot rows by 50cm. Increase the spacing between the two courgette plants to 90cm and 30cm from either end of their section.
- As the squash or pumpkins will happily expand to fit whatever space they are given, increase the length of Module 12 but don't alter the planting or spacings.

Garden plan: a mostly perennial kitchen garden

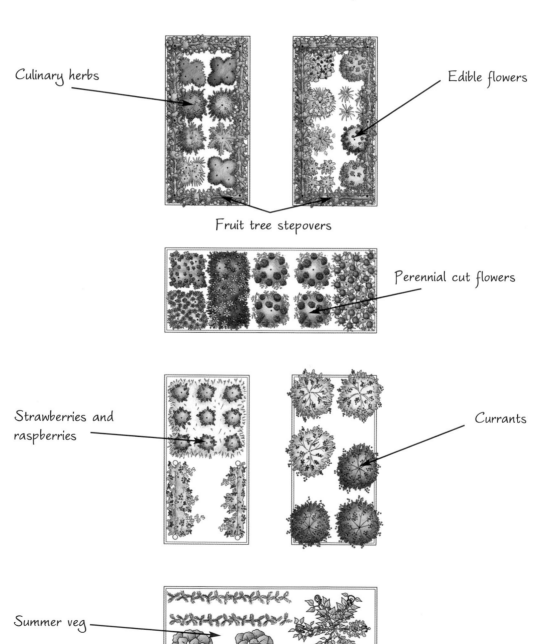

More salad veg

Culinary herbs

Edible flowers

Fruit tree stepovers

Perennial cut flowers

Strawberries and raspberries

Currants

Summer veg

Garden Plan: **A MOSTLY PERENNIAL KITCHEN GARDEN**

This kitchen garden has seven modules, so requires a little more space than other combinations. Using mostly perennial modules of herbs, edible flowers, cut flowers and fruit, with only two annual vegetable modules, it is a combination to use if you can afford the initial investment and intend to have the garden in the longer term, but can't commit a lot of time to it on a regular basis – you'd rather the plants just got on with it.

Modules in this garden

Module name (and number)	Size	Page reference
More salad veg (2)	2.5m x 1m	57
Culinary herbs (13)	2m x 1m	85
Edible flowers (16)	2m x 1m	91
Fruit tree stepovers (24)	2m x 1m	111
Perennial cut flowers (26)	2.5m x 1m	119
Strawberries and raspberries (18)	2m x 1m	99
Currants (22)	2m x 1m	107
Summer veg (3)	2.5m x 1m	59

Scaling up the modules
- For Module 2, extend the rows of lettuce and beetroot by 25cm each. This means you can station sow four lettuces per row, and just extend the drill for the beetroot.
- To increase the length of Module 26, add in another two rose bushes next to the existing ones.
- For Module 3, increase the length of the carrot rows by 50cm. Increase the spacing between the two courgette plants to 90cm and 30cm from either end of their section.

Garden plan: cut flowers and garnishes

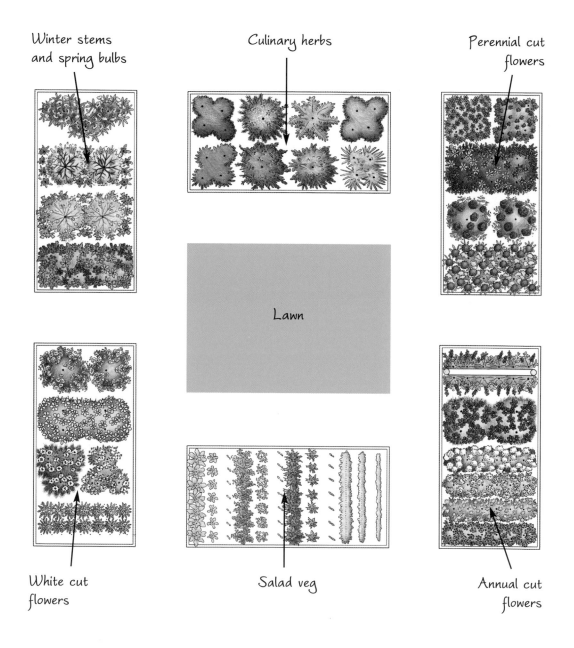

Winter stems and spring bulbs

Culinary herbs

Perennial cut flowers

Lawn

White cut flowers

Salad veg

Annual cut flowers

Garden Plan: **CUT FLOWERS AND GARNISHES**

This combination is intended to create a garden that can be enjoyed as a flower garden as well as a productive space. With a space for lawn in the middle, four of the six beds are of cut flowers, supplemented by culinary herbs to use either in the kitchen or in flower arrangements. The salad veg module is also included to give you some kitchen produce.

Modules in this garden

Module name (and number)	Size	Page reference
Culinary herbs (13)	2m x 1m	85
Perennial cut flowers (26)	2m x 1m	119
Annual cut flowers (25)	2m x 1m	117
Salad veg (1)	2m x 1m	55
White cut flowers (29)	2m x 1m	125
Winter stems and spring bulbs (27)	2m x 1m	121

Scaling up the modules
- No scaling up is needed in this plan, but if you have the space and wanted a larger lawn area in the middle, all the modules could be doubled in length.

Garden plan: garden produce and garden wildlife

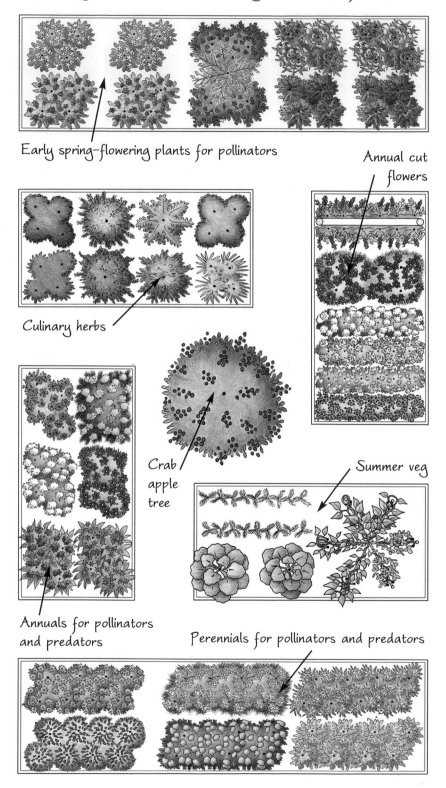

Early spring-flowering plants for pollinators

Annual cut flowers

Culinary herbs

Crab apple tree

Summer veg

Annuals for pollinators and predators

Perennials for pollinators and predators

Garden Plan: **GARDEN PRODUCE AND GARDEN WILDLIFE**

Attracting birds and insects is the central reason for creating this garden. However, there is also space for plants that are useful to you as well as the wildlife: bees will love the herbs, and bean and courgette flowers, and the annual cut flower module will also be rich in nectar for insects. To provide even more spring blossom you could add fruit tree stepovers to any of the perennial modules (aesthetically, either or both of the long perennial pollinators modules would be best).

The space in the middle of the plan could be left empty for a seating area, but a focal point of a crab apple tree has been included in the plan. Crab apples are extremely useful food sources for wildlife, both their flowers in the spring and the fruit for the birds in the autumn. You could also use some of the fruit to make crab apple jelly. Small trees, they require little to no pruning – only to remove dead or damaged branches – or any other maintenance. Two crab apples that are specifically listed on the RHS Plants for Pollinators list (see Further Reading) are *Malus* 'John Downie' and *Malus sargentii*, but most crab apples would be suitable, just check the ultimate height and spread.

Modules in this garden

Module name (and number)	Size	Page reference
Early spring-flowering plants for pollinators (32)	3.5m x 1m	135
Culinary herbs (13)	2m x 1m	85
Annual cut flowers (25)	2m x 1m	117
Summer veg (3)	2m x 1m	59
Annuals for pollinators and predators (30)	2m x 1m	131
Perennials for pollinators and predators (31)	3.5m x 1m	133

Scaling up the modules
- For Module 32, take each of the three sections in turn. Double the length and number of plants of the pulmonaria and primrose section and the bugle and hellebore section, making each 1.25m long. The middle willow section is increased to 1m long, but the number of plants is not increased, as the willow remains the centrepiece and the geraniums will happily spread to fill out the space.
- For Module 31, again treat it as a module of three sections. Add an extra 50cm onto the length of each section, which means there is space for another two plants in each.

Garden plan: a garden with sandy soil

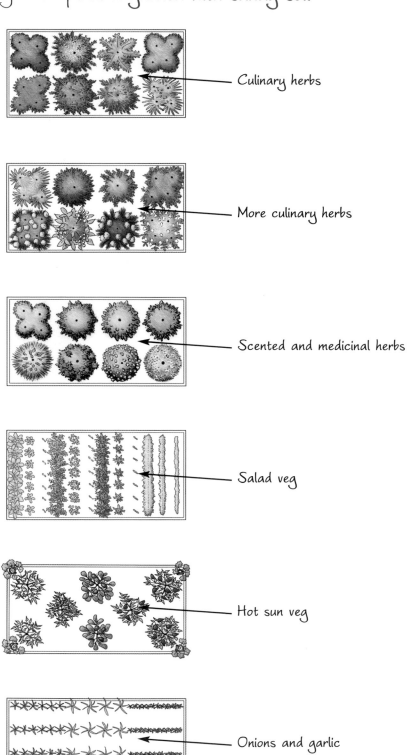

Culinary herbs

More culinary herbs

Scented and medicinal herbs

Salad veg

Hot sun veg

Onions and garlic

Garden Plan: **A GARDEN WITH SANDY SOIL**

Different plants are suited to different soil types. The modules in this combination contain plants that would be more suited to sandy soils, if you don't have the wherewithal to spend a lot of time improving the soil in the short term. Many herbs originate in the Mediterranean area, where they grow on very poor soil. In fact, the poor soil means that their oils and fragrance are more concentrated. Three herb modules are included here, and the other modules are of vegetables that will cope better in sandy soils, although they may need some more attention with the watering can in dry spells.

Modules in this garden

Module name (and number)	Size	Page reference
Culinary herbs (13)	2m x 1m	85
More culinary herbs (14)	2m x 1m	87
Scented and medicinal herbs (15)	2m x 1m	89
Salad veg (1)	2m x 1m	55
Hot sun veg (6)	2m x 1m	65
Onions and garlic (5)	2m x 1m	63

Garden plan: a garden with clay soil

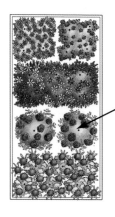

Perennial cut flowers

Squash and sweetcorn

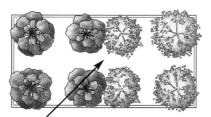

Rhubarb and gooseberries

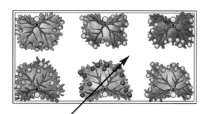

Fruit tree cordons

Garden Plan: **A GARDEN WITH CLAY SOIL**

The four modules in this combination are better suited to clay soil, but you are not limited to these alone. By improving the soil as explained in Chapter 4 you can plant most of the modules in this book. Fruit trees and bushes and perennial cut flowers will establish themselves and appreciate the clay's ability to retain more nutrients. The annual vegetables included are sweetcorn, whose deep roots will help break up the soil, and squash, which also improve the soil. Module 12 could be swapped for other vegetable modules in following years, but if your soil is very difficult to work, avoid anything that requires digging up, like potatoes.

Modules in this garden

Module name (and number)	Size	Page reference
Perennial cut flowers (26)	2m x 1m	119
Squash and sweetcorn (12)	2m x 1m	77
Rhubarb and gooseberries (21)	2m x 1m	105
Fruit tree cordons (23)	2m x 1m	109

Chapter 4
CREATING THE BEDS

CONSTRUCTING VEGETABLE/FLOWER BEDS

The principles of well-prepared soil remain the same for all the modules, regardless of size. If you have very sandy or very heavy clay soil, further remediation may be needed (see p. 41) and it is specified where the plants may require a slight variation: for example, herbs prefer well-drained soil.

Measuring out your beds

This is easy enough with a tape measure. Mark out the shape with string tied to canes, spray paint, or lay out a hosepipe. Check your corners are right angles with a set square or by measuring out a 3-4-5 triangle. This handy rule states that a right angled triangle with sides of 3m and 4m will have a hypotenuse of 5m. The rule is the same for any unit of length or multiples, e.g. 6-8-10, so check the corners of a standard 1m by 2m module bed with a 30–40–50 cm triangle.

Creating beds in a current lawn

You have two options: spray off the grass with herbicide such as 'Roundup', wait for it to die, then dig over the bed, or remove the grass and its roots from the top of the bed. The latter is more work, but allows you to get going and plant straight away.

   If you remove the grass, you can either incorporate it in strips in the bottom of your trenches as you dig (see Single digging, p. 40), or stack the strips up so they rot down into compost. Put them (grass side down) into a heap, making sure the final outside layer covers all the green bits, otherwise these will just keep growing. The heap could further be covered with old carpet or sacking to exclude the light.

Creating beds in current flower beds or weedy waste ground

Less work than digging up the lawn. Again, you can spray off and then dig, or dig over, removing unwanted plants and weeds as you go. Either way, single digging incorporating lots of organic matter would be beneficial, especially if the soil has been compacted.

PREPARING AND CULTIVATING THE SOIL

There are two schools of thought when it comes to the soil. The traditionalists thoroughly dig over their plots every spring or autumn, incorporating organic matter such as compost or well-rotted manure. The 'no-dig' school (see Further Reading) eschew such methods, preferring to let the worms do all the work of taking the organic matter into the soil: they simply spread a layer of organic matter over the top of the bed at the beginning of every season. The argument is that digging ruins all the work of the soil organisms – worms, insects, bacteria and more – to build a structure within the top and subsoils that benefits them and the plants.

When putting in your new beds, especially into compacted ground/lawn, a thorough digging over, removing perennial weed roots and incorporating plenty of organic matter, is helpful. Thereafter, or if you are converting areas that have not suffered much compaction or weed infestation, you can dig or not dig. Spreading a layer of organic matter, then using a garden fork to turn it into the soil lightly, is a happy compromise. At the same time, plunging the fork into the soil as deep as it will go and giving it a good wiggle will aerate the soil.

Single digging

The best method to use is single digging. 'Single' refers to the fact that you are digging one spit (spade's length) deep.

Once your bed is marked out, spread a thick layer of organic matter over the top. Then dig out a trench across the width of the shorter side at one end. The trench should only be the width and depth of your spade. Put what you dig out into a wheelbarrow or on a (plastic) sheet to one side. Use a garden fork to aerate the bottom of the trench, pushing it down as far as it will go and rocking it back and forward to open up the soil.

Dig out the next trench, turning over all the soil and organic matter into the first one, and repeat the fork-wiggling. The soil in the third trench gets turned into the second and so on until you reach the other end. The soil from the first trench can now be tipped in here.

Any large weeds you come across should be removed as you dig, making sure you get all of the root out. Small weeds can be left to rot at the bottom of the trench. To incorporate grass, dig up the lawn in strips (called turves), slicing underneath the grass's roots by holding your spade almost horizontally and pushing it. Put the turves grass-side down at the bottom of the trench, and break them up with your spade before covering them with the soil. The grass will be killed off and rot down into nutrient-rich soil at the bottom of the trench. Add organic matter one trench at a time.

Levelling and the gardener's shuffle

After single digging, or even forking in organic matter, the soil will be broken up and look considerably more voluminous. It is full of lots of large air pockets, which, if left, will fill with water every time it rains. Any plant roots in those pockets will either dry out and die or drown and die, so it's important to consolidate the soil into a reasonably level bed.

Rake the bed roughly level. Don't spend too much time on it – the final levelling comes later. Now it's time for the gardener's shuffle. This method has been used for centuries as a great way to consolidate the soil and tone your legs and buttocks! Start in the corner of the bed. Keeping your feet together, shuffle along the soil, putting your weight on your heels. Cover the whole bed in rows to make sure you don't miss a spot.

Rake the surface level, removing large stones and breaking up any clumps. You may need to do another quick shuffle over the top if you have had to level out big lumps and dips – do it at right angles to your original shuffle – and rake it over again.

Your soil should be level, consolidated but not compacted by the time you're done. Take a moment to appreciate your work – beds full of bountiful plants are brilliant, but freshly tilled earth has its appeal too. All good gardening starts with good soil, and a newly prepared bed is a sign of a productive season about to start.

Additional preparation for sandy soils
The main problem with sandy soil is that water and nutrients drain out relatively quickly. Adding plenty of organic matter will improve its moisture and nutrient retention.

Additional preparation for clay soils
Clay soils hold on to water and nutrients very well, but can get waterlogged. In very hot weather they can also dry solid and crack. Digging to loosen up compaction and the incorporation of plenty of organic matter – both dug in and as a mulch – will help. Use bulky organic matter such as horse manure that still has bits of straw in it, or home-made compost still with bits of twigs and fibrous stems: this will help break up the clay clods better. This is much more effective than adding grit or gravel, which may improve drainage slightly but won't encourage the creation of better soil in the long term. Dig your soil in late autumn if you can, but don't level or consolidate until spring. The frost will penetrate and break up all the clay clods for you over the winter.

Looking after the soil year-on-year; green manures
Digging in organic matter (or layering it on top, depending on your stance) every year is the best way to look after your soil. Avoid treading on and compacting it wherever possible.

Nature abhors a vacuum: bare soil, if left, will quickly get covered in weeds. After harvesting your last crops for the season, consider sowing a green manure for the winter, to add nutrients and suppress weeds. Sow the seeds, let the plants grow up and then cut them down and dig them in (precise instructions for each type will be on the seed packet).

Bed edging and raised beds

You don't need to add edges to your beds, but they help contain the soil, which will be raised above ground level by adding organic matter. Planks of wood, thick tree branches or trunks, old railway sleepers and more are all possible – whatever you can spend or get your hands on. Just make sure any wood has not been treated with creosote or other chemicals that could leach into the soil. You only need to build raised beds if your soil is really poor, or you have no soil at all.

SOWING SEEDS

Sowing seeds direct into the ground

This is the easiest method, but also the riskiest. Poor germination can mean gappy rows, and the emerging seedlings are most vulnerable to slugs and other pests.

First, prepare your soil. After levelling and consolidating, use the rake to break down the top of the soil into fine crumbs, removing any stones and other debris. You want no clumps so large that a seed might not be able to push a shoot through, but not dust that will solidify into a sheet after rain (known as 'capping' the soil). Station or drill sow (see below) as appropriate. Label each row stating what you've sown and when: marking the other end of the row (especially when sowing successively) can also be useful.

Hardy annuals will germinate in spring and withstand low temperatures, so you can sow them direct outside. To get earlier flowers they can be started off inside or in a greenhouse, then hardened off (see p. 44) before planting out, but it's not essential.

Half-hardy annuals cannot be sown or planted outside without protection until all risk of frost has passed (usually May/June). They can be sown under cover before this, or sown direct in late spring/early summer.

Station sowing

Make a small hole about twice the depth of the size of the seed. Water the bottom of the hole, then drop in two or three seeds and cover with soil, firming gently. It's tempting to leave all the seedlings to grow into plants, on the assumption that more plants mean more flowers or veg. However, thin the clump to one plant, otherwise they will compete with each other, to the detriment of all. Keep some pot-sown plants in reserve if you are worried about losing your selected seedlings to pests.

Sowing in drills

Use the corner of the rake or a hoe to pull the soil into a shallow trench, about twice the depth of the size of the seed, and water the bottom. Sprinkle your seeds along the trench; sowing 'thinly' as specified on seed packets means about a centimetre between seeds, but there's no need to be too precise. Cover with soil and firm gently. This is your drill. Thin the seedlings to their final spacing depending on whether or not you want to eat the thinnings (e.g. baby carrots); see p. 51.

Sowing seeds in pots and trays

This needs more initial outlay in equipment, and a sunny space to put the pots and trays. Raising seeds under cover in trays lets you sow earlier than the soil allows, and means you won't have any gaps in the rows. It's not suitable for all seeds – root crops are best sown direct.

Sowing in module trays

Using small pots can be wasteful of compost. Trays to create your own plug plants (known as module/cell trays) are more economical. They come in various sizes; 40 cell/plugs will be sufficient for your needs. The trays tend to be quite flimsy, so get some more solid seed trays as well for your module inserts to fit into. If you want to cover your seedlings for warmth and/or protection you can also get individual lids to create a mini-greenhouse. All of these are available relatively cheaply in garden centres and supermarkets.

Overfill the tray with compost, tap it on the ground to shake it down into the corners and scrape off the excess. Water it carefully, using a rose or spray fitting on your can/hosepipe. Sow one or two seeds per module and then cover with a thin layer of compost using a garden sieve or old colander. Clean the excess from the edges.

Water regularly to keep the compost moist but not soggy, and thin your seedlings to the best one in each module/cell when their true leaves (see Glossary) appear. The gaps underneath the cell tray are perfect hiding places for slugs, so check regularly.

Sowing in guttering

An alternative, particularly useful for drill-sown crops like cut-and-come-again salad leaves, radishes, beetroot and peas, is to sow your seedlings in a length of guttering. Buy and cut your guttering to the length of the rows you want, and sow your seeds. Once they are growing away, slide the compost and seedlings into a trench in the ground as a ready-made row.

Potting on seedlings

Bigger plants are more likely to survive pest attacks, so you could grow them bigger under protection by putting them into small (9cm) pots after the module tray. Half-fill your pots with compost. Extract your plug plants from the cell tray, put in one per pot and fill around the edges with compost. Don't push down at the base of the stem as you may break the roots off. Tap the pot sharply as you put it down to help consolidate the compost around the plug. Water thoroughly. Plant them out when the roots are coming out of the bottom of the pot.

Seed potatoes

Potatoes are grown from specific potatoes known as 'seed potatoes'. Available from garden centres, catalogues and online, the potatoes are split into groups depending on when they are harvested and their ultimate size, with many varieties in each group.

First and second earlies are what are generally known as 'new' potatoes, and are the first to be harvested. Salad potatoes are also small, and waxy. Maincrop potatoes are grown longest, produce the largest tubers with the most culinary uses and store the best.

Chitting seed potatoes

Buy your seed potatoes early in the year and then chit them for a few weeks to give them a head start. (If you don't buy them till later, chitting can be bypassed.) Chitting is putting your seed potatoes in a cool, dry, light place to develop small shoots before they're planted. The shoots will develop from the 'eyes', in the same way as if you leave eating potatoes in the back of the cupboard for too long.

Keep your seed potatoes upright in old egg cartons. Put them on a windowsill in a cool room. Spray them with a weak solution of liquid seaweed once a week to keep them healthy and not too shrivelled. Plant out your seed potatoes in early to mid-spring, in a hole three times the depth of the seed potato, with the strongest shoot facing upwards. Fill in the hole firmly but carefully to avoid snapping the shoot off.

Earthing up

Earthing-up potato plants makes them produce more. Once the shoots are about 20cm above the soil, draw up soil around the bottom half of the stems. Repeat this when the shoots are again protruding by about 20cm (see photo p. 45). Potatoes need a lot of water, but only in their later stages (last 2–3 weeks) of growth. Too much water before this can mean lots of leaves but not many potatoes.

Planting out onion sets and garlic cloves

Scrape or dig out a shallow hole and push the set/clove into it with the pointy top upwards. Firm the soil around it, leaving only the tip sticking out of the soil.

Hardening off plants

Plants raised (or bought) in pots/trays under cover need to be gradually acclimatised to conditions outside to avoid setbacks in growth and/or damage. Start hardening-off once all risk of frost has passed. You only need to harden-off plants when there is a considerable difference between the temperature outside and wherever you're raising them.

Put your plants outside just for the daytime to start with – choose a warm, sunny day – and bring them back under cover overnight. Repeat this for at least a

week, then leave them out at night as well, under a sheet of horticultural fleece, for a week or so, then plant them out.

PLANTING TIMES AND METHODS

The recommended planting methods for different types of plants are explained below. Where a plant has special requirements that differ from this, it is detailed in the information for that module and the general information at the start of that module's chapter.

Planting trees and shrubs

Check the plant before you buy it: you want healthy stems, branches and leaves, but also a good rootball. The plant should be well-rooted within its pot, with roots to the edge and bottom of the pot. If there is lots of fresh compost around the edge of a rootball that's smaller than the pot, it's been recently potted-on and you are paying more money for a small plant in a big pot. Conversely, it could be root-bound, with its roots wound round and round inside the pot with hardly any compost. Plants like this should also be avoided, but if you have no choice you can tease out some of the roots before planting.

Dig your planting hole at least twice the size of the pot your tree/shrub is in, and make sure the base and sides are not compacted. Mycorrhizal fungi can help your tree/shrub get off to a better start. It's available in good garden centres as 'Rootgrow': follow the instructions on the pack.

Plant your tree/shrub so that the top of the root flare is at soil level. Firm in the soil around the rootball well, and water (at least a watering can's worth). Make sure no mulch is touching the stem as it may cause it to rot. Keep it well watered for a few weeks, longer if the weather is particularly dry. Stake it if necessary (see p. 160).

Planting herbaceous perennials

Perennials can be planted in spring or autumn, when the ground is (still) warm and there is usually enough rain to keep the soil moisture levels high enough for the plants to establish. Dig a hole about half as big again as the size of the pot, and plant so the top of the rootball is at soil level. Fill in the soil around it firmly: there must be good contact between the rootball and the soil or it will be unable to take up water. A tug on the stems shouldn't dislodge the plant. Keep it well watered until it's established. Stake it if necessary (p. 160).

Pot sizes, divided clumps

Smaller plants take longer to grow and fill out their allotted space, it will be longer before you can start using them, and they need more watering until they establish. Ideally, buy herbaceous perennials in 1, 1.5 or 2 litre pots. These are not so small that they will take ages to get going, or so big that they are really expensive.

You may be able to divide clumps of herbaceous perennials from friends' plants. Do this in spring or autumn. Dig up the plant and, using a spade or two forks, cut or pull off a clump. Make sure it has a reasonably equal stem to root ratio (err on the side of more roots). Wrap it in a plastic bag to conserve moisture, and plant as soon as possible. Check the rootball for roots of perennial weeds before you plant it and water well.

Planting bulbs

Plant bulbs in autumn. Dig a hole three times the size of the bulb deep. Put the bulb in with the root plate at the bottom (pointy bit upwards), and fill in the hole firmly.

Planting perennials by plunging pots

Frost-tender perennials such as dahlias and pelargoniums need protection until all risk of frost has passed, and are therefore not usually planted out into the garden until May/June. They can be plunged into the soil in their pots so they're easier to bring indoors in the winter. Porous terracotta is better than plastic, but they'll still need more watering.

This method can also be used for invasive plants such as mint. In this case, leave the lip of the pot protruding above soil level between 2 and 5cm to make it easier to snip off the creeping stolons as they grow over the edge.

Planting out plugs of annual plants

If you've bought plug plants, plant them out as soon as you can. If you've sown your own, they're ready to plant out when the roots start coming out of the bottom of the module tray.

Push the plugs up and out of the tray from underneath; never pull the delicate main stem. Plant and firm in gently to ensure good contact between the rootball and the soil. A tug on the leaves should not dislodge the rootball. Don't press down directly around the base of the stem as this may break the roots off. Water well after planting and until established.

Chapter 5
THE MODULES: VEGETABLES

WHY IT'S GOOD TO GROW VEGETABLES

You are probably reading this because you already know you want to grow some vegetables. In brief, then, the benefits of home-grown vegetables are threefold. First, they taste better. Many salad veg are grown in hydroponic systems (where their roots just dangle in a flow of water and nutrients) rather than soil. This can result in watery, tasteless food. Home-grown vegetables can be picked at peak ripeness, again unlike shop-bought food, and eaten straight away, before the sugars transform to starch. This also applies to the second benefit: they are more nutritious. Common sense is all that is needed to see that a vegetable harvested ripe and eaten soon after is going to have more nutritional value than one harvested unripe and stored for days or even months before it is consumed. Third, the opportunity for variety is much greater. Even when restricted by the seasons, unlike supermarkets who can ship in tomatoes in December and sprouts in July, the different vegetables, and varieties within those vegetables, that you can grow outstrips any greengrocer. Purple carrots and potatoes, white 'green' beans, tomatoes with tiger-stripes, the hottest or mildest chillies and more are all within reach of your plot.

CHOOSING WHAT VEGETABLES TO GROW

With all that variety in mind, how do you choose which varieties to grow? In some modules recommended varieties are specified, but in general it is up to you. You could choose types not readily available in the shops, such as the giant bulbs of elephant garlic rather than the usual type, or purple-podded French beans rather than the normal green. You may want to grow heirloom or heritage varieties (see Further Reading for sources of these seeds), or the modern F1 types, which have been bred for specific traits such as pest and disease resistance.

Seeds marked with the Royal Horticultural Society's Award of Garden Merit (AGM) have been tested for good all-round garden performance in extensive trials, and are a good bet if you are not sure which to choose. Otherwise, consider what qualities you value most: taste, size, pest/disease resistance, time to harvest or colour. Most seed companies pick out one of these to highlight for each of their varieties.

Remember, whichever varieties you choose, to make a note of the name on the label and in a notebook. That way you can get more of the same next year if it was good, or avoid it if it didn't turn out as you'd hoped.

CULTIVATION

Soil preparation
There is no need for any preparation above that detailed in Chapter 4.

Planting times and pot sizes
Buying vegetables as young plants
With the increasing popularity of 'growing your own', it is now possible to buy young plants of many vegetables from garden centres. The traditional sources of small vegetable plants are also still valid – car-boot fairs, markets and plant stalls – but with these you may not know the variety of what you are buying (always a blow when it turns out to be the most delicious thing you've ever eaten) or that they are disease-free. Young plants from garden centres have more of a guarantee on both these things, but a less personable transaction.

Not all vegetables are available as young plants, and they are more expensive plant-for-plant than a packet of seeds, but if you only need two courgette plants, you may consider it worthwhile buying them as plants rather than a packet of 20 seeds that you then have to sow and grow on. There is also less variety and choice in young plants than there is in seeds.

However, young plants put straight into the garden have a more instant aesthetic effect, and, as they have already passed the seedling stage of highest vulnerability to slugs and snails, are more likely to survive. If you are late putting in your beds or sowing seeds, they can also provide an instant catch-up, or replace lost seedlings.

When buying young vegetable plants, check them carefully. See that they are not too overcrowded and root-bound in their tray (most plants come in module trays) or pot. Check for signs of pest and disease: are the leaves discoloured, full of holes or covered in aphids? Have the salad leaves already bolted? Be aware, though, that biggest is not always best – shorter, bushy plants are a better purchase than tall, leggy ones as they are more robust and will provide more to harvest.

Finally, don't fall for the garden centres' marketing ploys. They will often stock young vegetable plants from very early in the season – too early in fact for you to plant them out. The plants are raised in heated greenhouses with supplementary lighting to get them to grow, but if you plant them out in your beds straightaway in March they are likely to suffer from the cold, short days and may even die. Refer to the details with each module plan in this book for the correct times for planting.

Pot sizes
Most young vegetable plants are supplied in module trays or small (9cm) pots. If you can afford it, buy plants in the larger modules or pots as they will be less susceptible to drying out once planted before they establish. Alternatively, grow from seed (see below).

The perennial vegetables will be supplied in 1 or 2 litre pots. Again, the bigger the plant you buy, the faster it will get to its proper size in your garden. Asparagus is sometimes supplied as bare crowns (i.e. just in a bag, not planted in a pot). This is fine so long as they are planted as soon as you get them and you make sure they are well watered until they establish.

Sowing vegetable seeds – using the seed packet for information

See Chapter 4 (p. 42) on how to sow seeds successfully. General sowing times are specified in the detail for each module plan, but use the seed packet for guidance on that particular variety. The packet should show when to sow the seeds, how long they are likely to take to germinate, and the time between sowing the seed and harvesting your first crops. This can vary widely between varieties, and some seed companies now sell specifically fast-growing varieties.

Successional sowing

It is possible to have too much of a good thing sometimes, and unless you have plenty of freezer space or a love of making chutney you will want to avoid having gluts of vegetables. However, experienced gardeners still get it wrong, and the weather can wreak havoc on your planning – so much so that there are whole books dedicated to what to do with all those courgettes (see Further Reading)!

The trick to avoiding gluts is to sow successionally. By sowing several short rows of, for example, beetroot, with two weeks between each sowing, they will mature and be ready to harvest over a longer period, and less will be wasted. Module details specify where this is a good idea. Write the date you sowed the row on its label, and put a note in your diary when you need to sow the next row.

Alternatively, only sow the next row when the previous one has reached a certain stage, usually small seedlings with their first true leaves. This is more useful when bad weather slows germination.

Make your last sowing in August – falling light levels and temperatures mean you are unlikely to get a decent crop from seeds sown later than this unless you can protect them. Sow the last row of slower-growing crops such as beetroot at the begining of August, but faster crops like salad leaves should still provide you with a harvest from a final row sown at the end of the month.

Spacings and thinning seedlings

If you are planting out young plants, simply follow the spacings on the module plan for the distance between each plant. When sowing seed direct, follow the module detail for whether it is best to sow in stations or in a drill. Either way, you will have sown more than one seed, and that results in thinning.

To thin station-sown seedlings, choose the best seedling to be left in. Remember, tallest is not necessarily best – choose a robust-looking, healthy seedling. Press down the soil very lightly around the seedlings as you pull out the others to ensure the roots of the one you want to keep aren't pulled out too.

Drill-sown seeds offer an opportunity to use baby vegetables. Beetroot, salads and carrots are all good sown in a drill, but not thinned until they have grown into substantial baby plants. The plants you pull out can then be eaten rather than wasted, and those you leave in will still go on to grow to their proper size.

HARVESTING VEGETABLES

Harvesting the thinnings (as above) is generally the earliest you can reap what you've sown. Again, the seed packet indicates how long it takes from sowing to harvesting.

For the above-ground vegetables, it is fairly obvious when these are ready to harvest. It's best to pick vegetables while they are still small – this applies particularly to courgettes and beans – to encourage more to be formed. In the case of courgettes, if you leave them on the plant it is astounding how fast they turn into marrows.

Other vegetables need to be left to mature and ripen on the plant as they only produce one lot of fruit, such as pumpkins/squashes, and sweetcorn. However, it is possible to pick some mature fruit that is not ripe and ripen it inside if it is the end of the season and the harvest is likely to be ruined by frosts. Put green tomatoes in a dark place, such as a drawer lined with newspaper, and they will soon turn red. Chillies and peppers can be picked and eaten green, orange or red – if they feel firm when given a gentle squeeze they are mature, but not ripe (and therefore sweetest) until they are red.

With crops growing under the soil, the only way to really know if they are ready is to dig them up. Use the seed packet to give you a rough idea, then try with one plant. The topgrowth can also be an indicator: potatoes are generally ready once they start flowering, while the foliage of onions starts to wither and brown.

When you are picking vegetables, take care not to pull up or damage the plant – cut off your veg if necessary. Dig up root crops with a garden fork, digging as deep as possible under the plants before levering them up carefully, gently pulling on the topgrowth at the same time. Be sure to get all of them out as well: they are perennials and can regenerate from bits of carrot or potato left in the ground, which may be unwelcome in the bed next year. Salad crops usually come up with only a hand fork, but if you are digging out plants in a drill, make sure the neighbouring plants' roots are not left exposed.

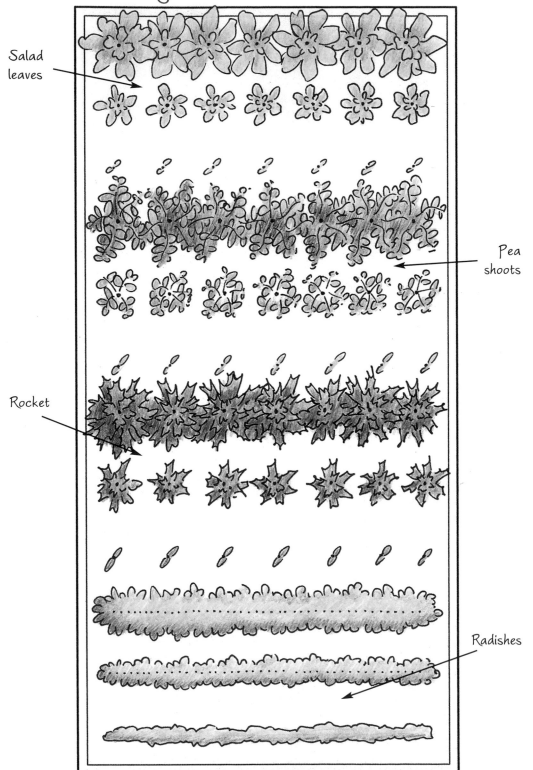

Salad leaves

Pea shoots

Rocket

Radishes

Module 1 **SALAD VEG**

This module is the most basic, and has the quickest return, of all the vegetable modules. Mixed baby salad leaves, rocket and pea shoots can all be cut soon after germination, and radishes are one of the fastest-growing vegetables. Do this module if you love to eat fresh salad every day, and want a variety of colours and tastes to your leaves.

Bed type: annuals

Plant name	Number needed	Potential yields
Salad leaves	Seed: 1-2 packets	20+ servings
Pea shoots	Seed: 1 packet	20+ servings
Rocket	Seed: 1-2 packets	20+ servings
Radishes	Seed: 1-2 packets	100+ radishes

Recommended varieties, planting and maintenance information
Salad leaves
- Any mixed salad leaves. The seed packet should state if they are suitable for cut-and-come-again (CCA). Different mixes are available such as mild or spicy leaves.
- Sow thinly in a drill according to packet instructions. Sow one row at a time, starting in March and leaving two or three weeks between each sowing to ensure a continuous supply. Once the first row is no longer producing well (usually after two cuts), remove the plants and re-sow, following with row 2 and so on.

Pea shoots
- Any pea seeds are suitable, but there are also varieties specifically for shoots.
- Sow as for salad leaves, but more thinly. Mice and voles may dig up the seeds: cover the ground with netting if you think they may be a problem.
- Use only the top few leaves as CCA then pull them out and re-sow.

Rocket
- Any culinary rocket seeds (not *Hesperis matronalis*, sweet rocket, which is an ornamental plant). Wild rocket has smaller and more bitter leaves than the cultivated.
- Sow as for salad leaves.

Radish
- Many different colours and shapes are available. Pick them small as larger radishes become woody and less tasty.
- Sow as for salad leaves.

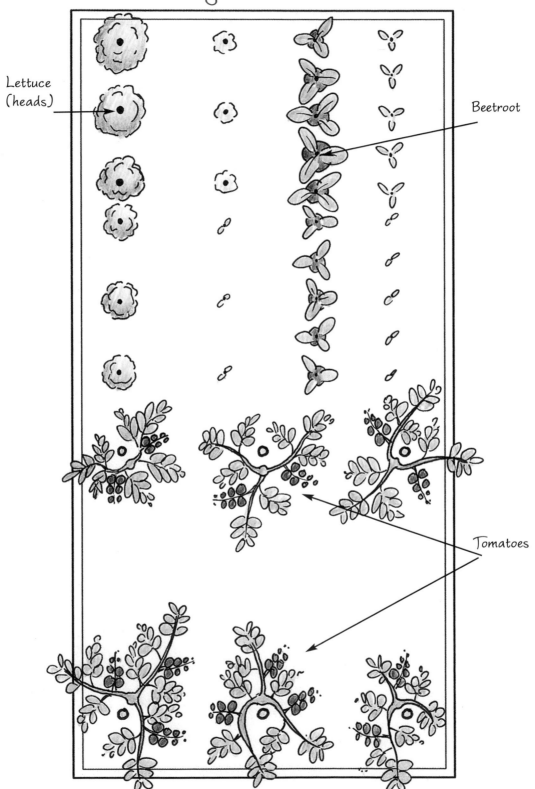

Lettuce
(heads)

Beetroot

Tomatoes

Module 2 **MORE SALAD VEG**

This module contains more substantial salad vegetables: whole heads of lettuce rather than just the baby leaves, plus beetroot and tomatoes (ideal for grazing on as you wander through the garden). All of these crops are vastly tastier than those available in the shops, and there is a great opportunity for growing different varieties.

Bed type: annuals

Plant name	Number needed	Potential yields
Lettuce (heads)	Seed: 1 packet per variety	12+ full heads
Beetroot	Seed: 1 packet per variety	20+ full size, more small
Tomatoes	Seed: 1 packet per variety or 6 young plants	10kg+

Recommended varieties, planting and maintenance information
Lettuce
- Head lettuce either forms a 'heart' (e.g. 'Little Gem') or doesn't (e.g. 'Salad Bowl', 'Lollo rossa'). Choose one or more types.
- Station sow three lettuces per row, sowing four rows successively overall. Keep plants well watered to avoid bolting. Harvest by either pulling up the whole plant and re-sowing, or cut, leaving a stump. It may resprout, but not a full head.

Beetroot
- Many different colours are available. 'Boltardy' has good bolting resistance.
- Sow four rows in succession from March onwards. Thin the rows and use as baby beets and re-sow rows after harvesting.

Tomatoes
- Cherry and smaller tomatoes are good for salads; plum and beefsteak types are better for cooking. Choose vine tomato plants for growing as cordons, not bush plants.
- Sow seeds under cover in March, or buy young plants; plant out in late spring (protect from frosts). Support with a stake and cut off the top of the plant when it reaches the top.
- Shoots forming in the axil of existing leaves on the main stem should be pinched or snapped off to make a single stem with leaves and fruit trusses and no other branches. Feed with a high-potassium liquid feed weekly once the plant starts to produce tomatoes.

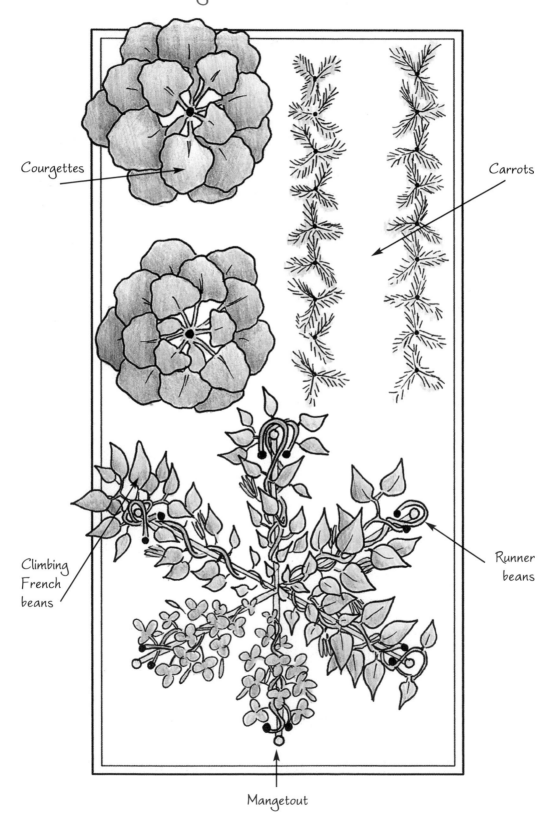

Courgettes

Carrots

Climbing
French
beans

Runner
beans

Mangetout

Module 3 **SUMMER VEG**

Classic veg plot staples for the summer – courgettes, carrots and climbing beans.

Bed type: annuals

Plant name	Number needed	Potential yields
Courgettes	Seed: 1 packet or 2 young plants	20+ courgettes, more small
Carrots	Seed: 1 packet	20–40 carrots plus thinnings
Runner beans	Seed: 1 packet or 4 young plants	1.2kg+
Climbing French beans	Seed: 1 packet or 4 young plants	0.8kg+
Mangetout	Seed: 1 packet or 4 young plants	0.2kg+

Recommended varieties, planting and maintenance information
Courgettes
- Green, yellow, cylindrical and spherical varieties available.
- Sow seed under cover in April/May, or buy young plants; plant out in late spring (protect from frosts). Water regularly.
- Harvest regularly for higher, tastier yields, rather than marrows.

Carrots
- Orange, purple and white varieties available, short, long or spherical. 'Resistafly' offers increased protection from carrot fly.
- Sow seed in a drill in March/April and thin. Sow successively or keep carrots in the soil until you're ready to use them. Mesh/fleece will guarantee protection from carrot fly.

Runner beans
- 'Scarlet Emperor' performs well, with long beans and bright flowers.
- Sow or plant two plants at the base of each of two canes of a six cane wigwam, in May/June. Wind the tendrils onto the cane to get them started. Pick regularly to avoid stringy beans and the plant going to seed.

Climbing French beans
- Round- or flat-podded climbing varieties available in green, yellow and purple (purple ones do not keep their colour when cooked).
- Sow and maintain as for runner beans.

Mangetout
- Green-, yellow- or purple-podded varieties available. Don't get a dwarf variety.
- Sow as for runner beans. Mangetout will not twirl round the canes, and will need tying in loosely every foot or so. Some extra twiggy bits at the base will help them get started.

Module 4 Spring and late summer veg

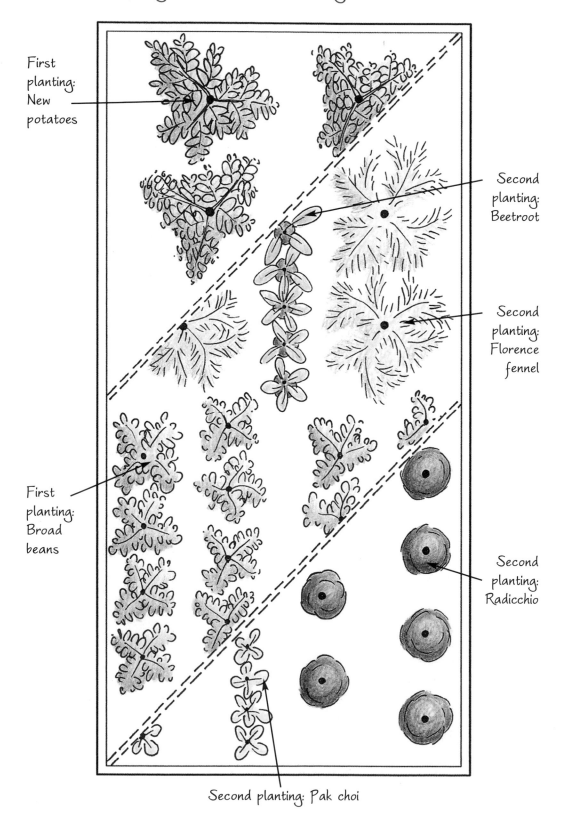

First planting: New potatoes

Second planting: Beetroot

Second planting: Florence fennel

First planting: Broad beans

Second planting: Radicchio

Second planting: Pak choi

Module 4 SPRING AND LATE SUMMER VEG

After a winter of stored vegetables, the fresh taste of broad beans and earthy new potatoes can't be beaten. The bed then gets used again for fast-growing crops that do better towards the end of the summer.

Bed type: annuals

Plant name	Number needed	Potential yields
New potatoes	6 seed potatoes	3kg+
Broad beans	Seed: 1 packet or 20 young plants	2–4kg+
Florence fennel	Seed: 1 packet	6 full bulbs, more small
Beetroot	Seed: 1 packet	10 full size, more small
Pak choi (bok choi)	Seed: 1 packet	20 whole heads, more CCA
Radicchio	Seed: 1 packet	10 full heads

Recommended varieties, planting and maintenance information

Potatoes: first planting
- Choose first earlies, e.g. fast-growing 'Rocket'.
- Chit and plant (see p. 44). Harvest three and a half months later.

Broad beans: first planting
- Dwarf plant 'The Sutton' crops well and is ideal for this module.
- Sow direct in late winter if it's not too wet, or under cover and plant out in early spring. Harvest when the beans in the pod are big enough. Pinch out the tops once the first flowers have set to encourage faster maturation.

Florence fennel: second planting
- 'Sirio' may be the only available variety.
- Sow direct as soon as the potatoes are out and the bed prepared again. Sow in six stations or sow in a drill and thin. Water well to prevent bolting.

Beetroot: second planting
- Available in many colours and sizes. 'Boltardy' has some bolting resistance.
- Sow 10 stations or in a drill and thin.

Pak choi: second planting
- 'Red Choi' (purple leaves), 'Choko' (green leaves), 'Ivory' (white midrib).
- Sow 20 stations or in a drill and thin. Use whole heads large or small or CCA. Water well to prevent bolting.

Radicchio: second planting
- Few varieties available: 'Palla Rossa Bella' may be the only one you can find.
- Station sow (10) when the beans are out.

Module 5 Onions and garlic

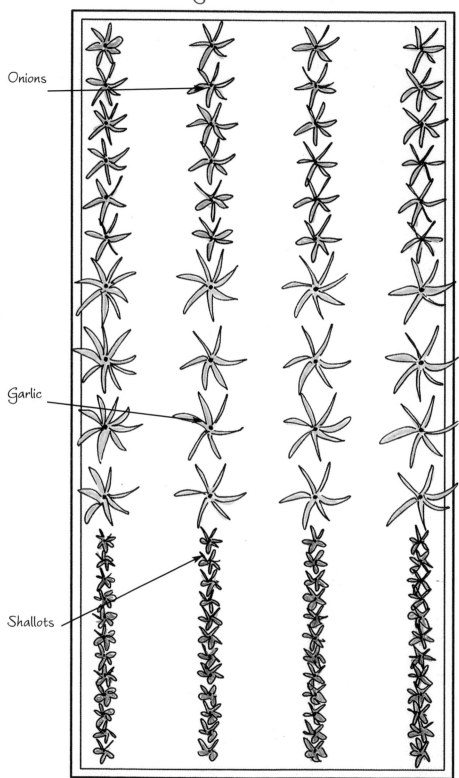

Onions

Garlic

Shallots

Module 5 **ONIONS AND GARLIC**

A very basic, very low maintenance module that will keep you in home-grown onions, shallots and garlic for some time. Dried and tied up in strings, they will keep well for months, or use the garlic green (fresh), which is rarely available in the shops.

Bed type: annuals

Plant name	Number needed	Potential yields
Onions	25–60 sets	25–60 onions
Garlic	16–20 cloves	16–20 bulbs
Shallots	50–60 sets	50–60 shallots

Recommended varieties, planting and maintenance information
Onions
- White or red varieties available.
- Plant out sets (see p. 44) in March, spaced 2.5–10cm apart, depending on how big you want the final onions to be. Keep weeds down, especially in the early stages, and cut out any flower stalks that are produced.
- Harvest when the tops start to flop over by pulling them up and drying them, preferably outside in sun, raised off the soil if you can (for example, on a chicken wire frame balanced on upturned flower pots). Once dry (the outer layers become papery like the onions you buy in the shops), string up and store in a cool place.

Garlic
- There are many different varieties: choose appropriate to the planting time.
- Plant cloves (see p. 44) 10–15cm apart in early winter if you can as they prefer a cold period to mature well, but spring (March) planting is also possible. Different varieties take more or less time to mature, but generally are ready to harvest in July when the bulbs have reached a good size. Use fresh or dry as for onions.

Shallots
- As for onions, but plant your sets 2.5cm apart as the final bulbs will be much smaller.

Module 6 Hot sun veg

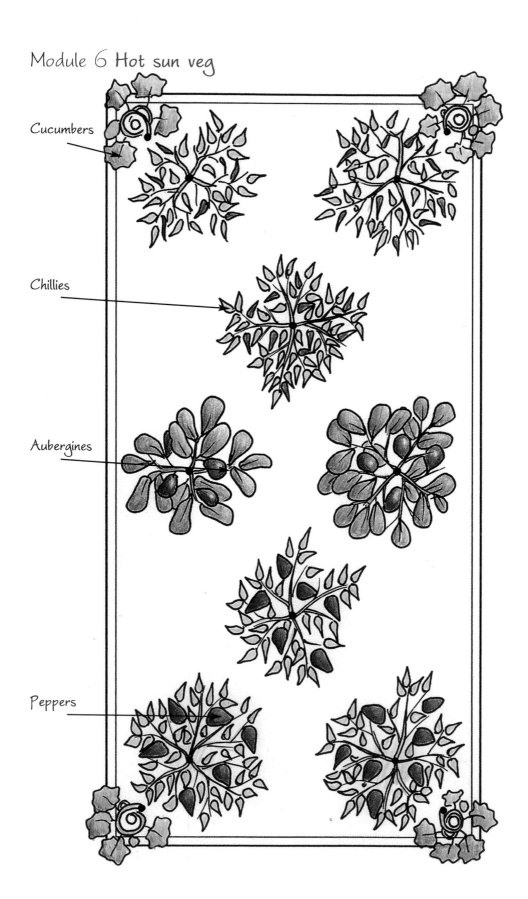

Cucumbers

Chillies

Aubergines

Peppers

Module 6 **HOT SUN VEG**

These veg need sun, shelter and warmth to grow and crop well, as they originate in countries much sunnier and hotter than the UK, but taste so different from shop-bought.

Bed type: annuals

Plant name	Number needed	Potential yields
Chillies	Seed: 1 packet or 3 young plants	0.75kg+
Aubergines	Seed: 1 packet or 2 young plants	1.2kg+
Cucumbers	Seed: 1 packet or 4 young plants	60+ cucumbers
Peppers	Seed: 1 packet or 3 young plants	0.75kg+

Recommended varieties, planting and maintenance information

In colder summers and at night all these plants will benefit from the extra heat under protective cloches or tunnels, but ventilate well during the day to prevent the plants scorching. All will need protecting from frosts.

Chillies
- Choose ones of a heat strength that you can actually eat!
- Sowing seed can be difficult and requires a heated propagator, so it's much easier to buy young plants. Plant out when all risk of frost has passed, and give them some support – tie in to a cane or spiral stake. They are ready to harvest when firm to a gentle squeeze (when still green), or wait for them to ripen to orange/red if you prefer.

Aubergines
- Sow and stake as for chillies. Pinching out the growing tip when you plant them out will make bushier growth that's easier to support. Aubergines are ready to harvest once they're dark purple.

Cucumbers
- Choose varieties selected for outdoor growing in the UK. The skins can be tougher than shop-bought ones, but they taste good.
- Sow seeds under cover in spring, or direct in early summer, or buy young plants. Tie in to a stake just under where fruit form to support the weight – not too tight as this will strangle the stem. Keep the ground moist to help prevent mildew. Pinch out the growing tip when it reaches the top of the cane. Pick regularly to encourage more to form.

Peppers
- As for chillies.

Asparagus

Globe artichoke

Module 7 PERMANENT VEG PLANTS

Permanent crops give a good reward for less input. Once planted, they can be left for many years – just reap the bounty. However, you will have to wait for a couple of years for the asparagus to get to a size where you can start harvesting.

Bed type: perennials

Plant name	Number needed	Potential annual yields
Asparagus	18 crowns	160+ spears
Globe artichoke	1 plant	5+ artichokes

Recommended varieties, planting and maintenance information
Asparagus
- Asparagus can be raised from seed, but takes even longer to establish, so buy crowns (usually one-year-old plants).
- Plant the crowns in spring on a small ridge (about 10cm above soil level), over a trench (about 30cm wide by 20cm deep) into which you have worked lots of organic matter. Spread out the roots and fill in with soil so only the bud tips are visible, then mulch.
- The plants will produce tall fronds of foliage in the summer: support these, then cut them back to 2.5cm above the ground once they start to yellow and die in the autumn. Mulch every spring. In the third year after planting you can harvest the spears for six weeks in spring (eight weeks in all following years), cutting them off below soil level.

Globe artichoke
- One plant doesn't seem much, but it will ultimately fill its part of the bed.
- Plant out in spring, and keep well-watered. The artichoke can be harvested from its first year in the ground, but will only produce one flower head (artichoke) in that year. Cut off when the scales are still green and about to open and the head is succulent and soft.
- In subsequent years the flower stem will have secondary flower buds, which can also be eaten, just below the main artichoke. Once the main one is harvested, leave the rest to mature, harvest, then cut the stem off at the base. In cold areas, protect the plant with fleece or straw over winter, and an extra layer of mulch around the base. Cut off dead leaves at the base.

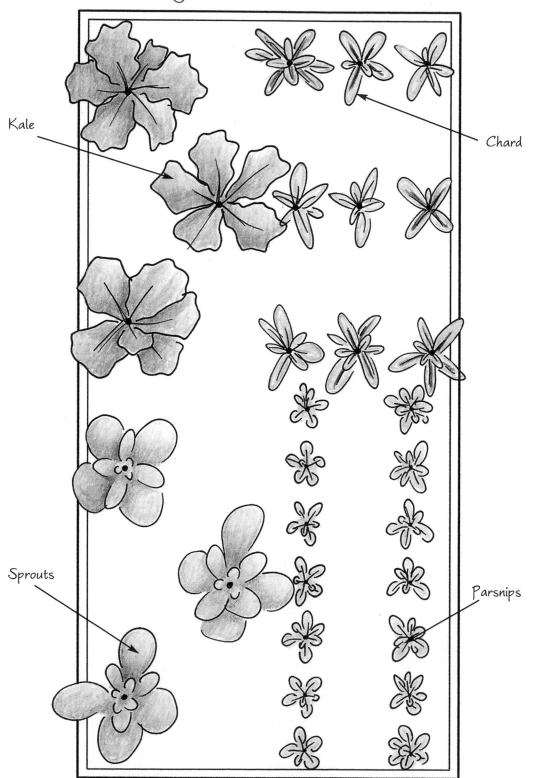

Kale

Chard

Sprouts

Parsnips

Module 8 **WINTER VEG**

This is one to do if you want to grow sprouts, parsnips and fresh leafy greens for your Christmas dinner. Chard is a good substitute for spinach, and kale chopped up and baked in the oven with oil and seasoning makes crispy 'seaweed'.

Bed type: annuals

Plant name	Number needed	Potential yields
Kale	Seed: 1 packet	1.8kg+
Chard	Seed: 1 packet	3.6kg+
Sprouts	Seed: 1 packet or 3 young plants	180+ sprouts
Parsnips	Seed: 1 packet	2.6kg+

Recommended varieties, planting and maintenance information
Kale
- Choose green or purple curly kale, or flatter, strap-like leaves with a larger central midrib.
- Sow direct or into modules in mid-spring and start harvesting in autumn, picking regularly to ensure a good supply of fresh young leaves. Remove yellowed leaves. Taller varieties may need staking.

Chard
- Available in single or multi coloured seed mixes – the mix 'Bright Lights' is attractive.
- Sow and harvest as for kale.

Sprouts
- For Christmas sprouts, choose winter-maturing varieties such as 'Wellington' (AGM).
- Sow and maintain as for kale. Harvest when the sprouts reach 2–3cm across. When the whole stem has been harvested, the rosette of leaves at the top can also be eaten.

Parsnips
- Choose a canker-resistant variety if possible, e.g. 'Tender and True' (AGM).
- Sow seed in a drill, or station sow, in mid- to late spring. Thin to 10–20cm between plants depending on how large you want your roots. Parsnip seeds take a long time to germinate so mark your rows clearly with labels, or mix with radish seed. The radish will germinate quickly to mark the row but be harvested before the parsnips get too big.
- Dig up your parsnips as you need them through the winter. They can suffer from carrot fly, so protect them in the summer if you want to. The foliage can cause a phytotoxic reaction on skin (like nettle rash), so use gloves.

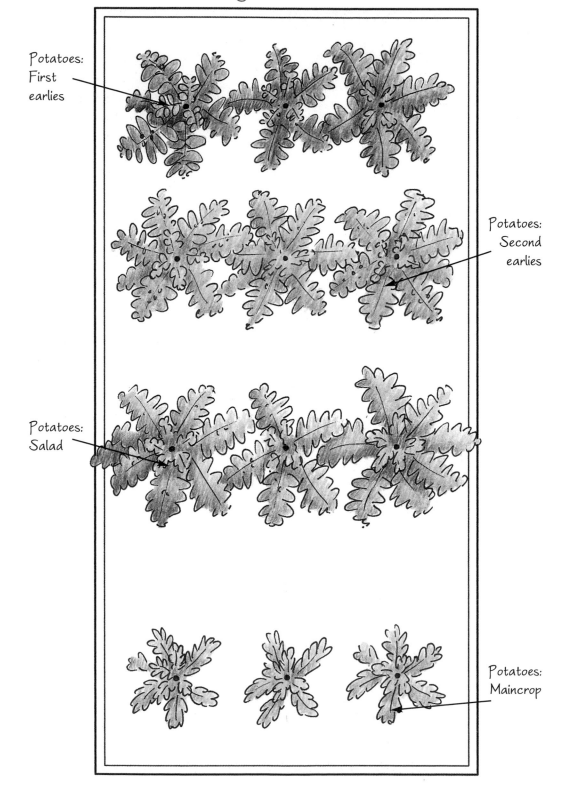

Potatoes:
First
earlies

Potatoes:
Second
earlies

Potatoes:
Salad

Potatoes:
Maincrop

Module 9 POTATOES THROUGH THE SEASON

Although potatoes are not the most expensive vegetable in the shops, growing your own offers all sorts of interesting varieties that are not widely available to buy, and the taste is generally far superior. They are also a great low-maintenance crop, as the foliage shades out most of the weeds, and all they need is some protection in spring against frosts. This module gives you fresh potatoes from the first 'new' potatoes through to larger ones in the summer for eating straight away or storing.

Bed type: annuals

Plant name	Number needed	Potential yields
Potatoes: first earlies	3 seed potatoes	1.5kg+
Potatoes: second earlies	3 seed potatoes	1.5kg+
Potatoes: salad	3 seed potatoes	1.5kg+
Potatoes: maincrop	3 seed potatoes	3.75kg+

Recommended varieties, planting and maintenance information
Potatoes
- Choose varieties most suited to your needs and tastes: online retailers and specialist potato fairs will offer more choice, particularly in heritage varieties, than garden centres.
- See p. 44 for information on planting and maintaining potatoes.
- Harvest first earlies 100–110 days after planting; second earlies and salad potatoes 110–120 days after planting; and maincrops 125–140 days after planting. All will keep in the soil (in frost-free conditions) until you are ready to use them, but will be susceptible to slugs, so lift and store them in a sack.

Peppers

Dwarf
French
beans

Carrots

Pak choi

Module 10 **STIR-FRY VEG**

This is the module to choose if you like your vegetables small and sweet. Harvest moments before cooking for the ultimate taste; stir-fry or add to a salad.

Bed type: annuals

Plant name	Number needed	Potential yields
Peppers	Seed: 1 packet or 3 young plants	0.75kg+
Dwarf French beans	Seed: 1 packet or 12 young plants	3kg+
Carrots	Seed: 1 packet	20+ carrots plus thinnings
Pak choi	Seed: 1 packet	12+ whole heads, more CCA

Recommended varieties, planting and maintenance information

Peppers
- Sowing seed can be difficult and requires a heated propagator, so it's much easier to buy young plants.
- Plant out when all risk of frost has passed, and give them some support – tie in to a cane or spiral stake. They are ready to harvest when firm to a gentle squeeze (when still green), or wait for them to ripen to orange/red if you prefer.

Dwarf French beans
- Purple and yellow varieties are available as well as the usual green.
- Sow in modules or direct in stations, thinning to the best seedling. Plants crop heavily when picked regularly, but for a shorter period than climbing varieties. Sow successionally if you want a regular supply. By protecting plants from frost you can harvest from May to October. Plants will need some support from small stakes.

Carrots
- Orange, purple and white varieties available, short, long or spherical. 'Resistafly' offers increased protection from carrot fly.
- Sow seed in a drill in March/April and thin. Sow successionally or keep carrots in the soil until you're ready to use them. Mesh/fleece will guarantee protection from carrot fly.

Pak choi
- 'Joi Choi' is bolt-resistant, 'Red Choi' has purple leaves.
- Station sow or sow in a drill and thin. Sow successionally to avoid the driest and warmest periods – some in spring under cover and planted out later, more in later summer. Use whole heads large or small or CCA. Water well to prevent bolting.

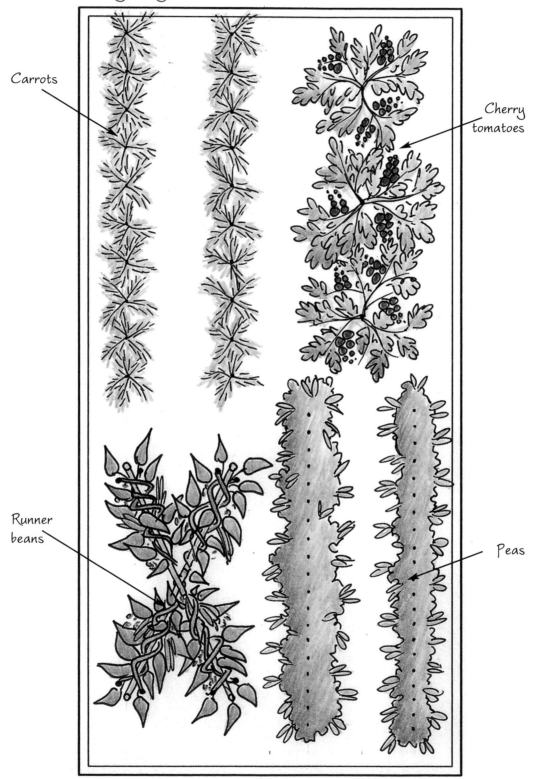

Carrots

Cherry tomatoes

Runner beans

Peas

Module 11 VEG TO GROW WITH CHILDREN

These are all veg that are good for encouraging children to get interested in vegetable gardening and eating. Cherry tomatoes plucked from the vine and peas straight from the pod can't be sweeter, and fast-growing runner beans can be raced to the top of the wigwam.

Bed type: annuals

Plant name	Number needed	Potential yields
Carrots	Seed: 1 packet	20+ carrots plus thinnings
Cherry tomatoes	Seed: 1 packet or 3 young plants	5.4kg+
Runner beans	Seed: 1 packet or 8 young plants	2.4kg+
Peas	Seed: 1 packet or 40 young plants	2kg+

Recommended varieties, planting and maintenance information
Carrots
- Orange, purple and white varieties available, short, long or spherical. 'Resistafly' offers increased protection from carrot fly.
- Sow seed in a drill in March/April and thin. Sow successionally or keep carrots in the soil until you're ready to use them. Mesh/fleece will guarantee protection from carrot fly.

Tomatoes
- 'Gardener's Delight' (red) and 'Sungold' (yellow) are both tasty and widely available. Choose vine tomato plants for growing as cordons, not bushes.
- Sow seeds under cover in March, or buy young plants; plant out in late spring (protect from frosts). Support with a stake and cut off the top of the plant when it reaches the top.
- Shoots forming in the axil of existing leaves on the main stem should be pinched or snapped off to make a single stem with leaves and fruit trusses and no other branches. Feed with a high-potassium liquid feed weekly once the plant starts to produce tomatoes.

Runner beans
- 'Scarlet Emperor' performs well, with long beans and bright flowers.
- Sow or plant two plants per cane in May/June, winding the tendrils onto the cane to get them started. Pick regularly to avoid stringy beans and the plant going to seed.

Peas
- Sow in modules in spring or buy young plants. Support with pea sticks or netting and water well as the plants flower and the pods start to swell.

Module 12 Squash and sweetcorn

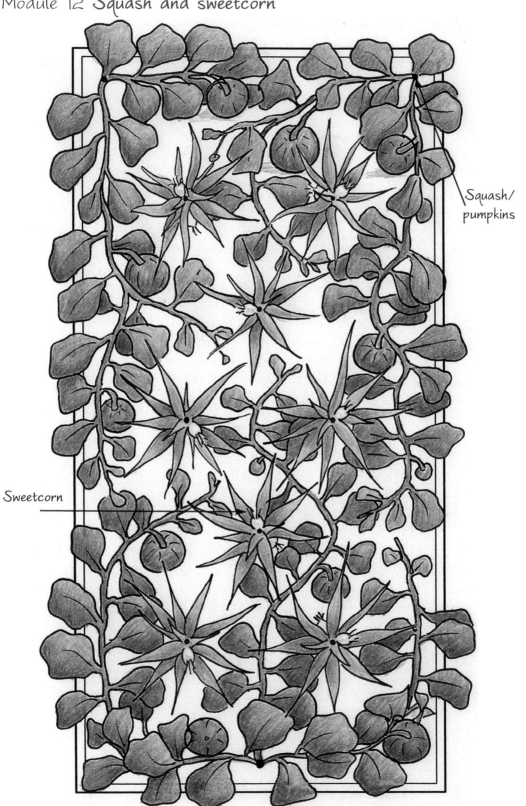

Squash/
pumpkins

Sweetcorn

Module 12 SQUASH AND SWEETCORN

Upright sweetcorn don't cast much shade over the squash scrambling over the ground underneath, which in turn shade out weeds. Squash is available in myriad shapes and colours, so go for less available types, or try for giant pumpkins. Sweetcorn on the cob straight off the plant tastes so different to even the freshest corn in the shops – have the water boiling and ready in the kitchen before you go and pick it to get the sweetest taste.

Bed type: annuals

Plant name	Number needed	Potential yields
Squash/pumpkins	Seed: 1 packet or 3 young plants	3 large/12–18 small fruits
Sweetcorn	Seed: 1 packet	8–16 cobs

Recommended varieties, planting and maintenance information
Squash/pumpkins
- 'Baby Bear' is a good small pumpkin; 'Crown Prince' is a tasty blue-skinned squash.
- Squash plants are frost-tender but require a long growing season, so sow under cover in mid-spring and plant out in May/June. Mulch around the base to conserve moisture. Use the sweetcorn plants or short stakes to direct the stems into and around the bed.
- Harvest when the squash/pumpkins have changed colour and sound hollow when tapped. Lift them off the soil with a pot or other supports as they ripen to prevent them from rotting in wet weather.

Sweetcorn
- 'Swift' is reliable with sweet kernels.
- Sow under cover in spring or direct in late spring: mini-cloches of half plastic bottles help warm the soil prior to sowing and during germination. Module-sown seeds benefit from deep pots for their long roots – loo-roll cardboard inners are ideal and can be planted tube and all. Earth up the base of the stems as the plants reach their final height to give them more support, but they shouldn't need staking. Cobs are ready to harvest when kernels, pierced with a knife or fingernail, exude a milky liquor. The tassels will have started to brown by then as an indicator.

Chapter 6
THE MODULES: HERBS AND EDIBLE FLOWERS

WHY IT'S GOOD TO GROW HERBS

Herbs are invaluable ingredients, with the power to transform a bland dish into something spectacular. Neither dried nor fresh herbs in the shops have the taste or potency of those just cut from the garden. Most everyday culinary herbs are easy to grow well in the UK.

Herbs are also renowned for their perfume. A combined scented and medicinal herbs module is included, but the culinary modules also provide their fair share of fragrance. Aromatic oregano, mint and lemon balm are brilliant for bulking out the showier blooms in posies of cut flowers.

The botanical Latin names of many herbs include the epithet '*officinalis*', which denotes them as a plant that was widely used by medieval apothecaries. Mainstream medicines still use synthesised versions of herb essences. Most herbs have healing properties attached to them, but the basic four in the medicinal herbs module are all suitable for the home doctor (consult a medical professional first).

The herb modules are also invaluable for attracting beneficial wildlife to your garden. If you do not have room for a Pollinators and Predators module (see Chapter 9, p. 127), a herb module will still help significantly. The powerful scent of many of these plants may also help to mask the smell of the fruit and vegetables you grow and thus deter pests such as carrot fly that find their food from the smell of the carrots. Herbs are also said to deter aphids. Hard scientific evidence for these effects is difficult to obtain, but it is common sense that a garden full of a diverse range of plants will attract a diverse range of wildlife that is most likely to keep the natural cycles of predator–prey relationships in balance.

Of course, it is not just the insects that will find your herb beds attractive – hopefully you will too. Through centuries of garden design, herbs have been one of the few constants. Although most of the herbs' flowers tend more towards the discreet than the showy, they are beautiful additions to a garden. The many types of foliage, some of them evergreen, also provide interest through the year.

WHY IT'S GOOD TO GROW EDIBLE FLOWERS

Edible flowers are becoming increasingly popular in restaurants, but to buy them can be very expensive (their delicacy means they must be fresh and harvested by hand). With a little effort you can have a plentiful fresh supply from these beds all summer. They can be used to give an interesting twist to savoury and sweet dishes, and to garnish drinks.

Module 16 contains those used mostly in savoury dishes, whose petals have citric or peppery flavours; Module 17 has flowers whose subtle scents are more suited to baked goods and sweets, but this is by no means prescriptive. Neither are these modules the extent of edible flowers – most herbs have edible flowers whose taste is generally a subtler version of their leaves. Some vegetable flowers are also edible, particularly those of courgettes, rocket and broad beans.

CULTIVATION

Soil preparation
Many of these plants originate from the Mediterranean, and prefer a free-draining soil. You can tell which plants have evolved to reduce water loss from their leaves: those with narrow leaves, silver colouring to reflect the sun, or a high oil content. They will tolerate cold temperatures, but need free-draining soil so that their roots don't rot in cold, wet ground. Prepare your soil appropriately (see Chapter 4, p.39).

Planting times and pot sizes
Refer to Chapter 4 for more information on planting or sowing. There are many varieties of herbs, with variegated leaves for example, or different growth forms. If possible, use the plants specified in the table for each module.

A cheap source of potted annual/biennial herbs is the supermarket. This works better for hardier herbs such as parsley than more tender basil, but by hardening them off properly (see p. 44) you can get decent crops. Supermarket herb pots often have more than one plant per pot, so you can divide it into two to four clumps that will each grow to a good size.

Maintenance
Let the plants grow into each other if you want, but a small border of space around each one will help air circulation (good for disease prevention) and weeding. All herbs benefit from regular trimming or cutting to keep them compact and bushy – use them regularly to achieve this. Specific care notes are included with each module; otherwise treat the herbs and edible flowers as befits their growth habit (see Chapter 11, p. 151).

HARVESTING HERBS

Cutting herbs for fresh use
When harvesting fresh herbs, cut the stems just above the next leaf or pair of leaves on the stem. The plant will re-sprout from the axils above the top leaves left on the stem; you're not left with an ugly stump which would then also be vulnerable to

infection. Consider the look of the plant as you harvest – take a little from each side. This regular harvesting will suffice as any pruning it may need, and also encourage bushier growth. When cutting the stems, taking off a third is a good rule of thumb.

Before using any herbs as a medicine or tea, be sure that you have got the correct plant. Check the botanical Latin names on the labels in the garden centre. The easiest way to use your herbs medicinally is to pick a few leaves, twist or tear them then pour on just-boiled water (it's best if it has gone off the boil to avoid scorching the leaves). The resulting tea will be infused with the herb's essential oils. This is ideal for peppermint, chamomile and lemon balm. A few fresh leaves of feverfew eaten daily is said to be efficient in preventing headaches and migraines. If you are in any doubt, consult your doctor or pharmacist before using the herbs.

Cutting herbs for dried use

Herbaceous herbs (e.g. mint, oregano and bergamot) can be dried to use in winter when fresh leaves are not available. The best time to cut them is in late May/early June, just before they start to flower, taking off around half of their growth. They will then have time to grow through the rest of the season to provide you with more fresh foliage and flowers.

If you can, cut them on an overcast morning after any rain or dew has dried. Tie the bases of the stems together with string and hang them upside down in a warm place until the leaves are completely dry. Pull off the leaves and store in an airtight container if using in the kitchen or for tea, or put into sachets or bowls if you are using them for scent.

For lavender, it is flowers that you need. Their dried scent is strongest if you cut them when the bottom rows of the flowers on each flower head are open, but the top ones have yet to bloom. Cut off the long stem where it changes from the more woody growth of last year to the softer stem of the current year's growth. This will be an effective prune of the plant as well, and it may put on a few more flowers before the year is out. Tie and hang the flowers to dry upside down; this preserves the colour of the flowers.

Collecting seeds for culinary use or for propagation
See p. 168.

HARVESTING EDIBLE FLOWERS

Flowers, once picked, will keep for 24 to 48 hours in an airtight container in the fridge, but they are best used fresh, so harvest them as you need them. Regular picking will prevent the plant from running to seed and encourage it to produce more flowers.

Pick flowers that are fully open but still fresh. The plant will more readily put on new growth if you cut off the flower stalk just above a leaf axil. You can cut or pinch the flower off the stalk in the kitchen later. When picking, put the flowers in a single layer in your box/basket – they are easily damaged. Shake each flower upside down and check carefully for any insects that might be lurking at the base of the petals.

Pick male flowers of courgettes (those without a baby courgette at their base) to avoid losing your veg; if your rocket is flowering then the leaves will be quite bitter, so the flowers are the best thing to eat anyway; remember with broad beans that if you pick a flower it won't produce a bean pod.

Module 13 Culinary herbs

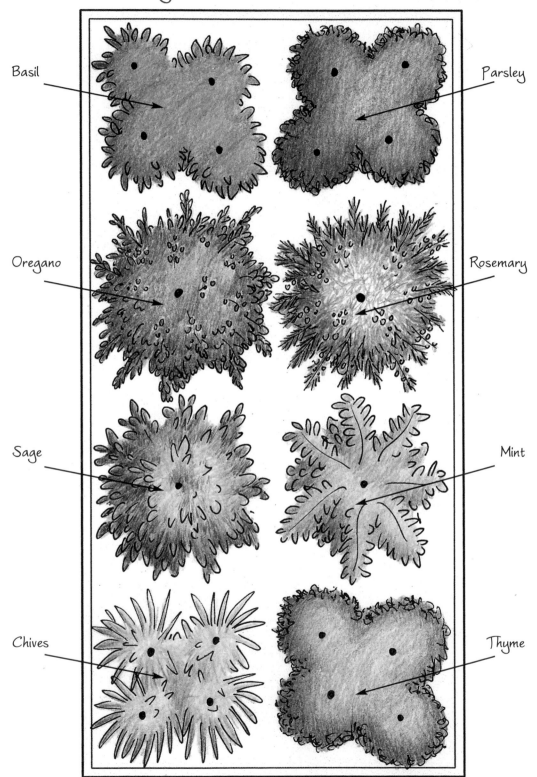

Basil

Parsley

Oregano

Rosemary

Sage

Mint

Chives

Thyme

Module 13 **CULINARY HERBS**

This module includes all the mainstays of the kitchen and is the easiest bed to plant and grow. Add fresh rosemary, thyme and sage to your roast dinners; basil, oregano, parsley and chives to your pasta sauce; and make fresh mint tea or mojitos all summer. Use these herbs to supplement your cut flowers too, especially oregano, mint and rosemary.

Bed type: mostly perennials

Plant name	Number needed	Growth habit
Basil (*Ocimum basilicum*)	4 (Seed: 1 packet)	Small bushy annual
Parsley (*Petroselinum crispum*)	4 (Seed: 1 packet)	Small bushy annual/biennial
Oregano (*Origanum vulgare*)	1 plant	Medium bushy herbaceous perennial
Rosemary (*Rosmarinus officinalis*)	1 plant	Large bushy evergreen shrub
Sage (*Salvia officinalis*)	1 plant	Medium bushy evergreen shrub
Mint (*Mentha spicata*)	1 plant	Medium bushy herbaceous perennial
Chives (*Allium schoenoprasum*)	4 plants	Small grassy herbaceous perennial
Thyme (*Thymus vulgaris*)	4 plants	Small prostrate evergreen shrub

Recommended varieties, planting and maintenance information
Basil and parsley
- Greek basil (*Ocimum minimum*) is much easier to grow from seed than ordinary basil (*Ocimum basilicum*), but you could use either.
- Sow your own for more robust plants, or buy from the supermarket or garden centre.

Chives and thyme
- Four plants are used per 50cm square to give you enough to start cutting them for use in the kitchen straightaway.

Oregano, rosemary and sage
- These will soon fill out their allocated space. Cut and use regularly to keep them to a decent size and to prevent them from becoming straggly.

Mint
- Mint spreads quickly by creeping rhizomes, so it's best planted in a plunged pot (see p. 47).

Module 14 More culinary herbs

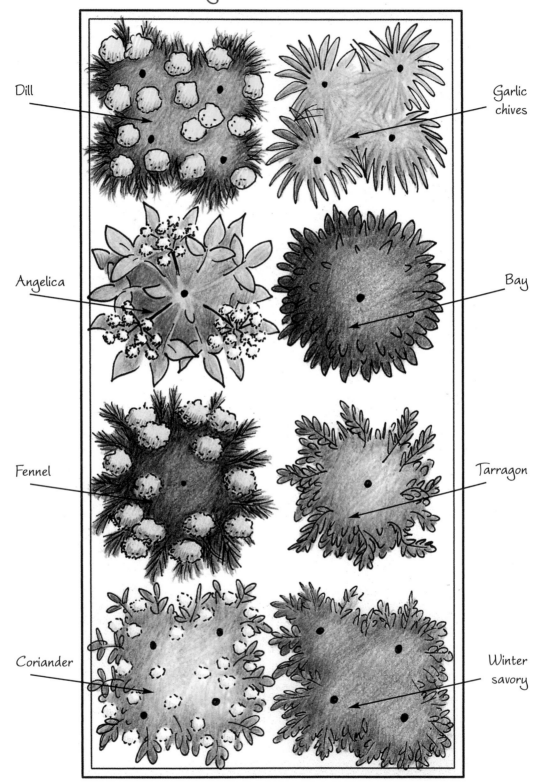

Dill

Garlic chives

Angelica

Bay

Fennel

Tarragon

Coriander

Winter savory

Module 14 **MORE CULINARY HERBS**

This module contains herbs that the more adventurous cook may use: bay and savory for soups and stews; fennel and dill with fish; and angelica for sweet dishes and candied flowers. Tarragon, coriander and garlic chives are also included as a supplement to Module 13 Culinary Herbs.

Bed type: mostly perennials

Plant name	Number needed	Growth habit
Dill (*Anethum graveolens*)	4 (Seed: 1 packet)	Medium upright annual
Garlic chives (*Allium tuberosum*)	4 plants	Medium grassy herbaceous perennial
Angelica (*Angelica archangelica*)	1 plant	Large upright biennial
Bay (*Laurus nobilis*)	1 plant	Large bushy evergreen shrub
Fennel (*Foeniculum vulgare*)	1 plant	Large upright herbaceous perennial
Tarragon (*Artemisia dracunculus*)	1 plant	Medium bushy herbaceous perennial
Coriander (*Coriandrum sativum*)	4 (Seed: 1 packet)	Small bushy annual
Winter savory (*Satureja montana*)	4 plants	Small bushy evergreen shrub

Recommended varieties, planting and maintenance information
Dill and coriander
- Grow from seed or buy young plants. Coriander is best sown successionally as it is prone to bolting, but use the seeds in the kitchen if it does.

Bay
- This can ultimately grow into a tree, but with regular trimming of shoots can be easily kept to whatever size and shape you want.

Garlic chives, tarragon, winter savory
- No special requirements.

Angelica
- This will grow as a herbaceous perennial for two (i.e. a biennial) to four years, but in that time will only put on leaves and no flowers. Once it has flowered it will die and needs to be replaced with a fresh plant. It's therefore advisable to sow some fresh seeds every year to have a little stock of plants at different stages, thus supplying you with flowers every year to use. It can also self-seed widely if allowed, providing you with more free plants. Plants bought from the garden centre are likely to flower that year or the next.
- May need staking.

Fennel
- May need staking.

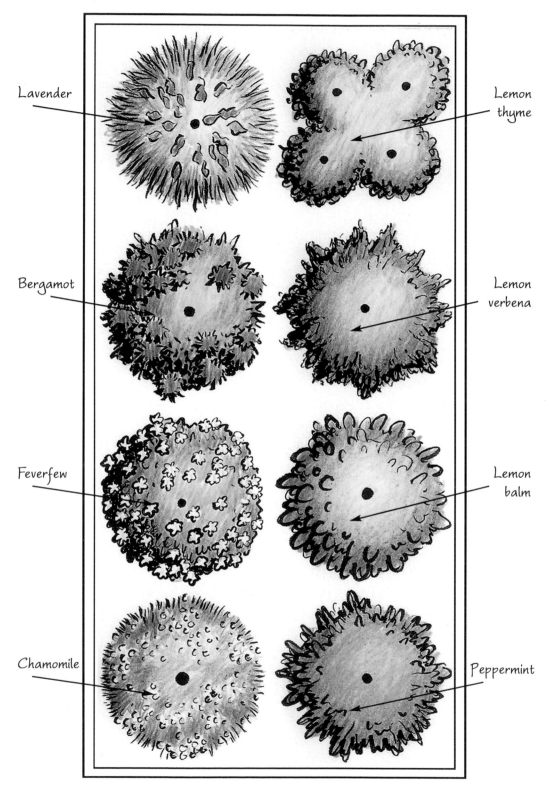

Lavender

Lemon thyme

Bergamot

Lemon verbena

Feverfew

Lemon balm

Chamomile

Peppermint

Module 15 SCENTED AND MEDICAL HERBS

Although this module includes herbs specifically selected for their scent and medicinal properties, all herbs have strong scents, and most have at least one beneficial property. Those included here are the most useful for home remedies and tea-making, and have the strongest aromas suitable for scenting the home, either fresh or dried.

Bed type: perennials

Plant name	Number needed	Growth habit
Lavender (*Lavandula angustifolia*)	1 plant	Medium bushy evergreen shrub
Lemon thyme (*Thymus citriodorus*)	4 plants	Small bushy evergreen shrub
Bergamot (*Monarda didyma*)	1 plant	Medium bushy herbaceous perennial
Lemon verbena (*Aloysia citrodora*)	1 plant	Medium bushy deciduous shrub
Feverfew (*Tanacetum parthenium*)	1 plant	Medium bushy herbaceous perennial
Lemon balm (*Melissa officinalis*)	1 plant	Medium bushy herbaceous perennial
Chamomile (*Chamaemelum nobile*)	1 plant	Small prostrate evergreen shrub
Peppermint (*Mentha* x *piperita*)	1 plant	Medium bushy herbaceous perennial

Recommended varieties, planting and maintenance information
Peppermint
- This will spread as garden mint does, so it is best planted in a plunged pot (see p. 47).

Lemon verbena
- This is not always fully hardy in the UK. Protect your plant through the winter with a mulch of organic matter around the base of the plant to insulate the roots, and cover the top growth with horticultural fleece or a large cloche as soon as frosts start in the winter. It may not put on new leaves until summer. Alternatively, plant it in a plunged pot, moving it inside in its pot for the winter.
- Prune in spring to a framework of main stems about 30cm long, taking side-shoots back to two or three buds and removing the 4Ds (see p. 165).

Others
- No special planting or maintenance requirements.

Module 16 Edible Flowers

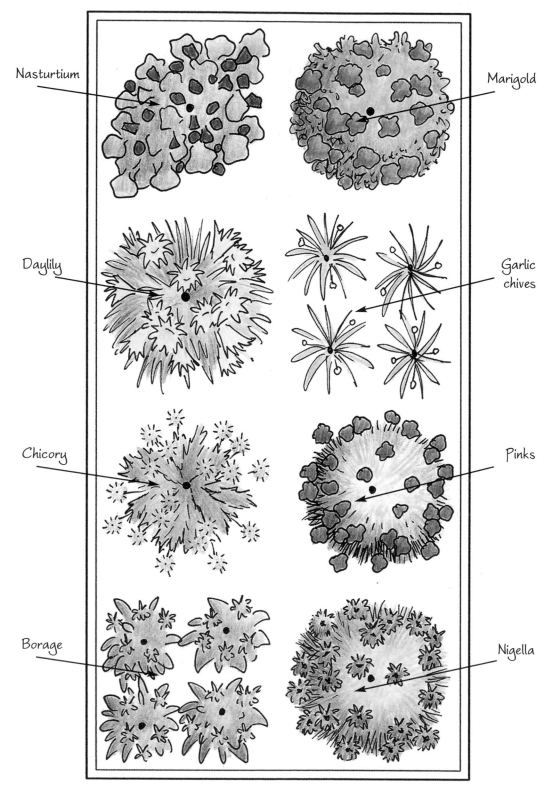

Nasturtium

Marigold

Daylily

Garlic chives

Chicory

Pinks

Borage

Nigella

Module 16 EDIBLE FLOWERS

This bed includes a variety of flowers that will all add a colourful dimension to savoury dishes. Most have a delicate peppery flavour. Nigella is also included for its herby, mustard-like seeds, which are used in many ethnic dishes. Use the flowers in salads, or as garnishes, and freeze borage flowers in ice cubes for adding to cocktails. Nasturtium seeds can also be pickled into mock 'capers'.

Bed type: perennials and annuals

Plant name	Number needed	Growth habit
Nasturtium (*Tropaeolum majus*)	1 (Seed: 1 packet)	Rambling annual
Marigold (*Calendula officinalis*)	1 (Seed: 1 packet)	Bushy annual
Daylily (*Hemerocallis lilioasphodelus*)	1 plant	Grassy herbaceous perennial
Garlic chives (*Allium tuberosum*)	4 plants	Grassy herbaceous perennial
Chicory (*Cichorium intybus*)	1 (Seed: 1 packet)	Upright herbaceous perennial
Pinks/carnation (*Dianthus caryophyllus*)	1 plant	Bushy herbaceous perennial
Borage (*Borago officinalis*)	4 (Seed: 1 packet)	Upright annual
Nigella (*Nigella damascena*)	1 (Seed: 1 packet)	Bushy annual

Recommended varieties, planting and maintenance information
- Where possible, stick to the straight species of all of these plants, as given above. However, varieties, for example of the daylily, would also be fine. If you prefer flowers of a particular colour, for example of the nasturtiums, it would also be fine to choose a variety instead, but be sure to check the height and spread of the plant, given the space restrictions.

Nasturtium, marigold, nigella, borage and chicory
- Sow seeds in spring according to the packet. Remove plants when they have died in the autumn (except chicory: just cut off dead topgrowth).

Garlic chives, daylily and pinks/carnation
- Plant in spring. Cut back dead foliage in spring/autumn.

Nigella
- Pinch out the very top of each shoot/stem when the plant is small to encourage more stems and therefore flowers. Leave the flowers and wait for the seedheads to form before harvesting and drying the seeds (see p. 168).

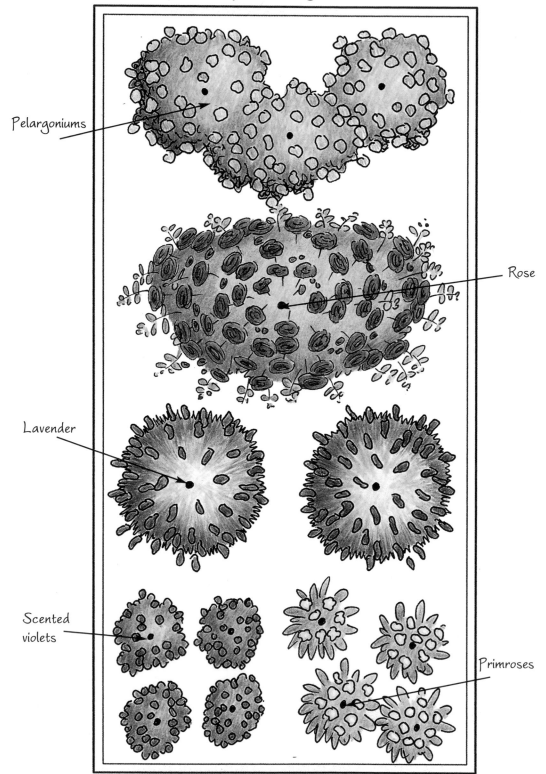

Pelargoniums

Rose

Lavender

Scented violets

Primroses

Module 17 EDIBLE FLOWERS FOR BAKING

This bed contains the edible flowers more commonly used for sweets and baked goods: lavender for flavouring cakes and sugar; rose for its petals and hips; pelargoniums for their highly perfumed leaves; and scented violets and primroses to crystallise for decorations. Many of these can also be used to make flavoured syrups, sugar or waters.

Bed type: perennials

Plant name	Number needed	Growth type
Pelargoniums, scented (*Pelargonium*)	3 plants	Medium bushy perennial/shrub
Rose (*Rosa gallica* var. *officinalis*)	1 plant	Medium bushy shrub
Lavender (*Lavandula angustifolia*)	2 plants	Medium bushy shrub
Scented violets (*Viola odorata*)	4 plants	Small bushy perennial
Primroses (*Primula vulgaris*)	4 plants	Small bushy perennial

Recommended varieties, planting and maintenance information

Pelargonium
- There are hundreds of different-scented pelargoniums, from lemon to cinnamon, nutmeg to cedar and talcum powder – choose the culinary scents you like.
- These are not hardy in the UK. Plant in plunged pots that can be brought in for the winter, or buy new every year. Cut back to a good framework of stems about 10cm from the base every spring.

Rose
- The variety recommended here, known as the apothecary's rose, fits the space with a spread of 1m. However, if you are expanding this bed you could use a larger rose such as the damask rose (*Rosa* x *damascena*). Both have fragrant flowers and good hips, but the apothecary rose's scent is stronger.
- Does not require heavy pruning. Remove the 3Ds (see p. 165) and trim off old hips in early spring before the buds start to break.

Lavender
- When harvesting, cut the stems to just above where they change from soft to woody. Cut back any stems left in the same way in late summer.

Scented violets and primroses
- Pick the flowers regularly to encourage more, or deadhead if you've not used them. Remove dead leaves. Otherwise, they need no maintenance.

Chapter 7
THE MODULES: FRUIT

WHY IT'S GOOD TO GROW FRUIT

There is nothing like spying a ripe fruit as you wander through the garden, and munching it there and then. Fully ripe and warmed by the sun, freshly-picked fruit is so much more delicious than chilled, under-ripe, anaemic supermarket offerings.

Fruit is also less work than vegetables. Once planted, the bushes or trees will keep producing year on year. The pruning can be off-putting, but it's really not complicated and quite difficult to go drastically wrong. Even if it does, you're very unlikely to kill the plant, and it will probably still produce fruit for you next year. Buying fruit trees and bushes is more initial outlay than for vegetable seeds, and is a longer-term commitment (apart from strawberries), but by adding modules gradually you can stagger the expenditure.

Fruit trees and bushes are also good for wildlife, as they flower quite early in the season and their woody structure gives shelter to insects over winter. Of course, the birds will also love your fruit, but some simple netting at the critical ripening time will protect your harvest.

Choosing varieties

The choice of varieties of fruit is smaller than that of vegetables in the garden centres, but online retailers can offer a wider range. Some fruits need pairing with specific plants to ensure good pollination, while others are not fussy. It is specified in each module where you need to be careful what you choose.

CULTIVATION

Soil preparation

Prepare the soil as normal (see Chapter 4, p. 39). Shrubs and trees will need plenty of space for their roots to spread so make sure your soil, if it's compacted, is properly dug over.

Planting times and pot sizes

Planting shrubs and trees is best done in early autumn, if possible, as it will give your plants time to establish before they have to start flowering and fruiting in the spring and summer.

Strawberries are generally supplied growing in pots or large module trays, and these should be planted out in autumn or early spring. You may be able to get rooted runners from a friend or a plant stall in autumn.

Rhubarb crowns are best planted when they are dormant in autumn to mid-winter, but try to plant when the soil is warm and not too wet.

Staking and netting

Young fruit trees, whether they are trained as cordons or stepovers, will need staking to prevent them getting damaged in windy weather (see p. 161).

Netting your soft-fruit crops is not necessary – you could use bird-scarers – but if you don't want to see your harvest decimated it is advisable. Large-scale cages are expensive, but some hazel or bamboo canes, some netting and string will also do the job, and you can remove them once the fruit is harvested (see p. 162).

Pruning

Pruning your fruit trees and bushes is not something to be scared of. The modules use the most straightforward trained forms: the cordon, stepover and bush. In essence you are cutting back the branches to restrict the tree's growth to a size and form you want, and to encourage the plant to make flowers and fruit, not lots of leaves. Pruning takes place in summer and/or winter. See the module details for when you should be pruning your plants and what form they are grown in.

How you prune your fruit trees and bushes does depend on how old they are, though, and while the basics are outlined in each module, there is not space to do the topic justice. See Further Reading for sources of information such as online advice.

Thinning

In a good year for pollination, the fruit of apples, pears and plums can get overcrowded on the branch. To get good-sized fruits (rather than a cluster of under-sized ones), thin your developing fruits in early July, making sure you have finished by mid-July. The tree may do most of the work for you in June, shedding a number of baby fruits, a process known as the June drop. Choose one fruit (the best one) per cluster to leave on apples and pears, removing the rest. On plums, keep the best fruit, leaving one or two every 10cm or so.

HARVESTING FRUIT

Currants and berries

These are the easiest to tell when they are ripe – they change colour and are soft to the squeeze. Other indications are fruit dropping to the ground, and the birds/squirrels trying to eat them. Depending on your varieties, this could be anywhere between June and September.

Gooseberries can be picked unripe for cooking with, but if you want to eat them raw, wait until they are ripe or they will be incredibly sour. Pull them carefully off the branches. Red- and blackcurrants are attached to the stem on a little string or stalk: it's easiest to snap off the whole string where it joins the main stem and then tidy them up later.

Likewise, snap off a bit of the strawberry stem rather than pulling the fruit off the hull – it will keep better, and it avoids rot developing on the remaining hull that might spread to unharvested fruit. Conversely, raspberries are ripe when they can be easily pulled off the hull.

Apples, pears and plums

Plums turn colour and are soft when squeezed when they are ripe in July or August. Lift the fruit carefully upwards and its stalk should separate easily from the tree branch.

Apples and pears will also lift off easily from the branch when ripe. As this can be any time from August to November, check the label of the trees you buy. If you have to pull at the fruit to get it off the branch, it isn't ripe. You'll also start seeing windfalls as an indication.

Rhubarb

Rhubarb should not be harvested for the first year after planting to allow the crown to establish: by pulling the stalks and leaves off you are removing its ability to photosynthesise. The following year, don't take more than a third of the stems. From the third year onwards you can either harvest relatively heavily in the early part of the year as the first stems come up, or pull a few regularly from spring to late summer. Stalks are ready to harvest when they are 23–30cm long and pull away easily from the crown: hold the stalk near the base and give it a gentle tug. Don't cut it if it won't come away naturally. The leaves are not edible.

You can also force established rhubarb (year three onwards) for very pink, tender stems in early spring. Cover the crown in mid-winter with a layer of straw or dry leaves (clear away old stems first), then cover with an upturned pot, bucket or traditional terracotta forcing jar. Exclude all light by covering any holes in the bottom of the pot. Blanched stems can be harvested two or three weeks ahead of the usual picking time – wait until they have reached the top of the pot/bucket before pulling them as above. Once done, forcing cannot be repeated on the same crown the following year, as the plant needs time to recover.

Module 18 Strawberries and raspberries

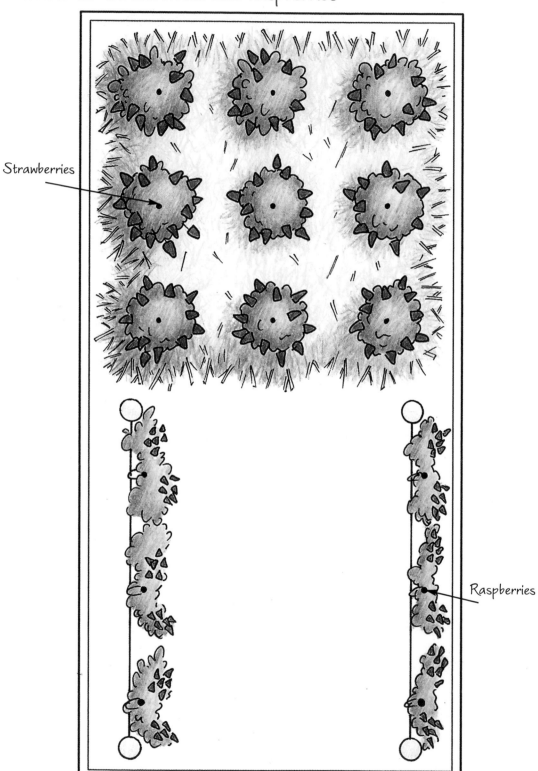

Strawberries

Raspberries

Module 18 STRAWBERRIES AND RASPBERRIES

A good introduction to fruit-growing: enough strawberries and raspberries for summer desserts and jugs of Pimms.

Bed type: perennials

Plant name	Number needed	Potential yields
Strawberries	9 plants	4kg+
Raspberries	6 plants	4kg+

Recommended varieties, planting and maintenance information
Strawberries

- Available in early, mid- and late season varieties, and perpetual plants that fruit steadily all summer. 'Honeoye' (early), 'Cambridge Favourite' (mid) and 'Rhapsody' (late) all have AGM. 'Bolero' and 'Viva Rosa' (perpetual) are recommended.
- Plant in autumn or early spring. The 'crown' should be at soil level: too deep and it will rot, too high and it won't establish well. Remove dead leaves and fruit stalks in spring. Surrounding your plants with straw will keep the fruit off the soil but can harbour slugs.
- If you don't want to propagate your own plants, cut runners off to the base. However, strawberry plants are best replaced every three years, and runners are free. Plant the first mini-plant on each runner in a small pot and leave it, still attached to the main plant, until autumn, watering as required. Cut off the runner beyond that first mini-plant: subsequent ones on the same runner will be weaker and reduce the vigour of the first. In autumn, detach it from the main plant and grow it on ready to plant out in spring.

Raspberries

- Summer-fruiting raspberries have early, mid- and late season varieties. 'Glen Moy' (early), 'Glen Ample' (mid) and 'Leo' (late) all have an RHS AGM.
- Once you have put in your stakes and wires (see p. 162), plant your raspberry canes in autumn or spring. Tie in the canes to each wire.
- Summer-fruiting raspberries produce fruit on the canes grown the previous year, so in the summer the plants will have both old fruiting canes and new canes. In autumn, cut back canes that had fruit on them to ground level. Also cut out any new canes that are smaller than pencil thickness. Tie in all the new canes.

Module 19 Strawberries through the season

Strawberries

Module 19 STRAWBERRIES THROUGH THE SEASON

By dedicating a whole bed to strawberries you have enough plants to get a decent harvest in the early, mid and late parts of the season. If you want to preserve the fruit as jam or ice cream, choose only one or two fruiting seasons to make sure you have the quantities all at once.

Bed type: perennials

Plant name	Number needed	Potential yields
Strawberries	18	8kg+

Recommended varieties, planting and maintenance information
Strawberries
- 'Honeoye' (early), 'Cambridge Favourite' (mid), 'Rhapsody' (late) all have an AGM. 'Bolero' and 'Viva Rosa' are recommended perpetual fruiters that will produce fewer fruit at a time but flower and fruit steadily through the summer.
- Plant out potted strawberries in autumn or early spring, making sure the 'crown' of the plant is at the same level as the soil: too deep and it will rot, too high and it will struggle to establish. Remove dead leaves and fruit stalks in spring. Surrounding your plants with straw will help keep the fruit off the soil, but may harbour slugs. Plastic sheeting restricts the ability of water to get to the roots and is not recommended.
- Strawberry plants produce runners – long stalks on which small plants form, ready to root and grow where they touch the ground. If you don't want to propagate your own plants, cut these off as they appear. However, as strawberry plants are best replaced every three years, it is a free source of new plants. Plant the first mini-plant on each runner in a small pot filled with compost and leave it there, still attached to the main plant, until autumn, watering as required. Cut off the runner after that first plant: subsequent mini-plants on the same runner will be weaker and reduce the vigour of your first potted one. In autumn, detach it from the main plant and grow it on ready to plant out the following year.

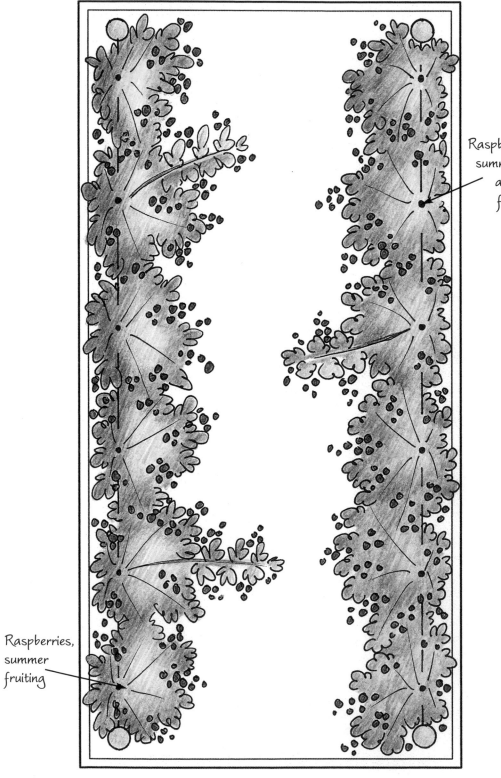

Raspberries,
summer or
autumn
fruiting

Raspberries,
summer
fruiting

Module 20 RASPBERRIES THROUGH THE SEASON

This module offers you higher yields of raspberries than the mixed strawberry/raspberry module, and also offers the opportunity to split your harvest between summer- and autumn-fruiting raspberries. Autumn-fruiting varieties don't yield as much fruit per plant as the summer-fruiting types, but the luxury of fresh raspberries up until the first frosts is worth the smaller harvests. Plant all the same or one row of each.

Bed type: perennials

Plant name	Number needed	Potential yields
Raspberries, summer fruiting	6 plants	4kg+
Raspberries, autumn fruiting	6 plants	2kg+

Recommended varieties, planting and maintenance information
Raspberries, summer fruiting

- Summer-fruiting raspberries have many early, mid- and late season varieties. 'Glen Moy' (early), 'Glen Ample' (mid) and 'Leo' (late) all have an AGM.
- Once you have put in your stakes and wires (see p. 162), plant your raspberry canes in autumn or spring. Tie in the canes to each wire to prevent them from falling over and wind damage.
- Summer-fruiting raspberries produce fruit on the canes grown the previous year, so in the summer the plants will have both old fruiting canes and new canes without fruit. In autumn, cut back the old fruited canes to ground level and any new canes that are smaller than pencil thickness. Tie in the new canes.

Raspberries, autumn fruiting

- 'Autumn Bliss' has an AGM and is the best and most commonly available variety.
- Plant and stake in the same way as summer-fruiting raspberries, and tie in the canes.
- Cut back all the canes to soil level in February: new shoots will be produced in spring which will fruit that year. In mild areas, where frosts are less likely to damage fruit, cut out canes as soon as you pick the last raspberries from them. More canes will then produce fruit and you can pick into late autumn and winter.

Module 21 Rhubarb and gooseberries

Rhubarb

Gooseberries

Module 21 **RHUBARB AND GOOSEBERRIES**

A module of early-season tartness. Rhubarb is very easy to grow – just plant the crowns and reap the harvest. Gooseberries require a little pruning to keep to a decent size but otherwise are very forgiving plants. Both will tolerate some shade.

Bed type: perennials (herbaceous and shrubs)

Plant name	Number needed	Potential yields
Rhubarb	4 crowns	4.5kg+
Gooseberries	4 bushes	14kg+

Recommended varieties, planting and maintenance information
Rhubarb
- 'Early Champagne' produces sweet stems early in the season, while 'Victoria' is later with heavy yields.
- Plant out potted crowns with the top of the pot compost level with the soil surface. Mulch them in spring, but do not cover the top of the crown as it will rot. Keep well-watered in dry spells, and remove dead or yellowing leaves through the season. If a flower spike is produced, cut it off at the base as it will reduce the vigour of the crown.
- Force and/or harvest as required (see p. 97). A rotation of one forced plant in four could be established in the third year. Remove all dead foliage at the end of the season.

Gooseberries
- 'Careless' (culinary) is early-fruiting, 'Invicta' (culinary) high-yielding, 'Leveller' (dessert) is yellow in colour and has a good flavour, and 'Whinham's Industry' (culinary/dessert) is red. All have an AGM.
- Gooseberries need good drainage. The flowers are produced in early spring and can be damaged by frosts, so don't plant in a frost pocket, and fleece flowering plants if heavy frosts are forecast.
- Prune for a bush form in winter/spring before the plants come into leaf. Either use the renewal method, taking out a third of the oldest stems to their base to create an open-centred goblet shape, or spur-prune. Spur-pruning aims to keep the framework of main branches the same, and removes sideshoots to within two or three buds from the main branch. The main branch is also shortened by about a third to restrict the size. With either method, remove the 4Ds too (see p. 165).

Module 22 Currants

Redcurrants

Blackcurrants

Module 22 **CURRANTS**

Shiny currants look like strings of jewels hidden beneath the leaves. Another relatively low-maintenance module, this is fruit that is not easily available in quantity in the shops. Blackcurrant leaves also make a delicious tea.

Bed type: perennials (shrubs)

Plant name	Number needed	Potential yields
Redcurrants	3 shrubs	12kg+
Blackcurrant 'Ben Sarek'	3 shrubs	13.5kg+

Recommended varieties, planting and maintenance information
Redcurrants
- White and pink currants are also available and are grown in the same way. Redcurrants 'Jonkheer van Tets', 'Stanza' and 'Red Lake' all hold an AGM for good yields.
- Plant potted or bare-root plants in autumn or spring in well-drained soil.
- Prune in a bush form in winter/spring before the plants come into leaf. Either use the renewal method, taking out a third of the oldest stems to their base to create an open-centred goblet shape, or spur-prune. Spur-pruning aims to keep the framework of main branches the same, and removes sideshoots to within two or three buds from the main branch. The main branch is also shortened by about a third to restrict the size. With either method, remove the 4Ds first (see p. 165).

Blackcurrants
- 'Ben Sarek' is a dwarf form more suited to the size of this bed. Ensure your plants are certified as virus-free – blackcurrants are especially disease-prone.
- Plant in autumn or spring, using potted or bare-root plants. Unlike all other plants, blackcurrants benefit from being planted deeply in the soil, with the base of the plant buried around 5cm below the soil level. This will stimulate the production of new shoots.
- Stems may need staking to prevent them breaking under the weight of the fruit.
- Pruning is straightforward and aims to keep the bush open and upright. Take out the 4Ds first (see p. 165), then any further stems to balance out the bush, removing around a quarter of the stems in total. Cut them back to 2.5cm from soil level in winter/spring before the plants come into leaf.

Module 23 Fruit tree cordons

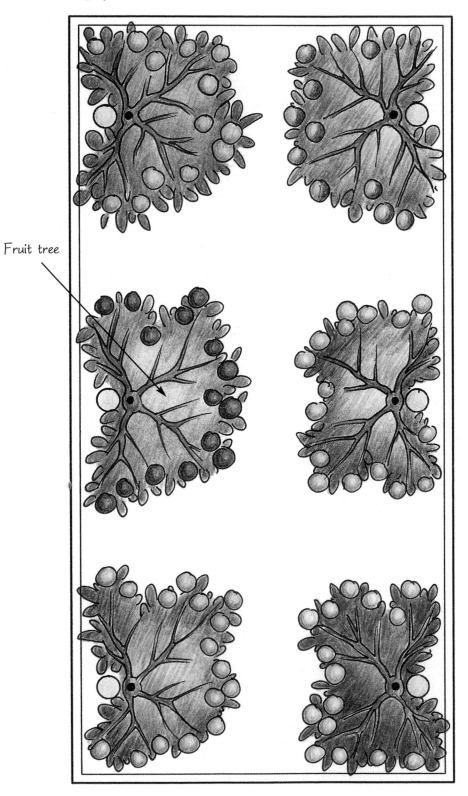

Fruit tree

Module 23 FRUIT TREE CORDONS

You don't need space for a huge fruit tree, as you can get a surprising quantity of fruit off a compact trained form. The easiest form is the vertical cordon (minarette), essentially a free-standing column with very short side branches.

Bed type: trees

Plant name	Number needed	Potential yields
Apples, pears or plums	6 young trees	13kg+ apples; 10kg+ pears; 21kg plums

Recommended varieties, planting and maintenance information

Stake your trees (see p. 161).

Apples
- Buy trees within the same or next pollination group (see Glossary) so at least two trees are flowering at the same time. M27, M9 or M26 rootstocks (see Glossary) are all suitable. Ballerina types, of which there are a limited number of different fruit varieties, are bred to grow in vertical columns and require less pruning.
- Plant one- or two-year-old trees (maiden whip/feathered maiden) in late autumn or winter.
- Prune after planting to take any side-shoots back to three buds. In the summer reduce the side-shoots again to three buds and in the winter cut the main stem/trunk back by a third of its height until it reaches its final height of 2–2.5m.

Pears
- As with apples, choose varieties from the same pollination group, and on dwarfing rootstock Quince C.
- Plant and prune as for apples.

Plums
- There is less choice for plums. Pixy is the best rootstock, on which you should be able to find self-fertile stalwarts such as 'Czar' and 'Opal'. Check the pollination group of other varieties. Where possible buy a feathered maiden (two-year-old tree).
- Plant as for apples.
- Prune in the first spring after planting, cutting back all side-shoots to three buds and the main stem/trunk by half, or to above the highest side-shoot, whichever is topmost. In the summer cut back side-shoots again to six buds/leaves. If they continue growing, cut back the new growth to one leaf of the previous cut. In late summer cut the shortened side-shoots back to three buds of the main stem. In following springs, reduce the main stem/trunk by a third of its new growth and side-shoots as for the first year.

Module 24 Fruit tree stepovers

Fruit tree

Module 24 FRUIT TREE STEPOVERS

Stepovers means just that – trees are trained horizontally along a wire a couple of feet off the ground so you can step over it. Use this module around another module as a pretty and productive fence edging. It's best used with a module that is completely or mostly perennials – the digging up and planting of annuals every year would cause too much disturbance to the stepovers' roots.

Bed type: trees

Plant name	Number needed	Potential yields
Apples or pears	6 young trees	13kg+ apples; 10kg+ pears

Recommended varieties, planting and maintenance information

Set up your stakes and wires first (see p. 162)

Apples

- Buy trees within the same or next pollination group (see Glossary) so at least two trees are flowering at the same time. M27, M9 or M26 rootstocks (see Glossary) are all suitable.
- Plant one-year-old trees (maiden whips) in late autumn or winter. Plant on the outside edge of the bed in front of the stakes. Secure the tree to the stake but leave it upright. In the spring (when the flowing sap makes the stem more pliable) gently bend each tree over until it can be tied in horizontally to the wire (tie it at several points along the stem). Tie each tree the same way – clockwise or anti-clockwise is your choice.
- Prune in the summer to reduce the side-shoots to three buds. Tie in the leader to the wire as required until it reaches the next tree, at which point cut off the tip. Treat any subsequent growth beyond the end tip as a side-shoot.

Pears

- As with apples, choose varieties from the same pollination group, and on dwarfing rootstock Quince C.
- Plant and prune as for apples.

Chapter 8
THE MODULES: CUT FLOWERS

WHY IT'S GOOD TO GROW CUT FLOWERS

If you buy cut flowers on a regular basis (or would like to), growing and cutting your own is cheaper and more sustainable. Flowers from your allotment or garden are much fresher, and can be cut at the right time for their best display. The variety of flowers that can be grown gives a wider choice than the florists and supermarkets, and is more seasonal. Flowers increase the biodiversity of your garden, and will attract pollinators and other beneficial insects.

Module 27 includes dogwood (*Cornus*) plants, whose red stems can be cut to use for Christmas decorations, and pussy willow (*Salix caprea*), with its furry catkins in spring. Both are increasingly available to buy as stems, but are relatively expensive compared with the cost of a plant that will produce stems year after year.

CULTIVATION

Soil preparation

Prepare the soil as normal (see Chapter 4, p 39). The plants will benefit from some cosseting. There is an impression that growing plants 'hard' (depriving them of water and nutrients) will make them flower. It's true that when a plant is stressed it will put all its energy into making flowers: it wants to reproduce because it thinks it is about to die. However, the flowers tend to be smaller and on short stems: just look at the difference between weeds growing in good soil and weeds growing in paving cracks. For large flowers on long stems, mulch, water and feed well.

Planting times and pot sizes

While general sowing and planting times have been detailed in Chapter 4 and in each module, the seed packet is a valuable source of information too. Check it for guidance on sowing times and techniques for that particular variety. The packet will also sometimes have a picture of the plant in its seedling stage, useful for distinguishing it from weeds.

Successional sowing

The annual flowers are all cut-and-come-again (CCA), so you don't need to sow successional batches to guarantee flowers over a long period, as the plant will do that for you. However, they will go over and die eventually, so by sowing two batches three to four weeks apart (within the sowing months specified on the packet), you can extend the season a little longer. This could be applied to sweet peas and cornflowers especially.

Within the overall group of bulbs – for example, daffodils – different varieties flower at different times of year, with a month or more between some varieties. Generally they are grouped into early, mid-, and late season varieties. Decide whether you want lots of flowers at the same time, or a few over a longer period, and choose accordingly: garden centres and online retailers should denote when a particular variety flowers.

Spacings

Cut-flower plants can be placed much closer together than if you were planting a normal border because by cutting them you are continually limiting their size. Normal spacings can be reduced by up to a third, reflected in the plan for each module.

HARVESTING CUT FLOWERS

As a general rule, the best time to cut the flowers is when the buds are opened enough that they are showing the colour of the petals, but not yet fully opened. If you cut them before they are showing colour they may not open at all. Some plants (e.g. *Eryngium*) can be cut as flowers, left to cut for seedhead displays later in the year, or a mixture of both. You may also enjoy seeing the colour of the flowers in the garden, and choose to leave some blooms in the bed rather than cutting them all for the house.

Harvesting seeds for sowing next year

For more on harvesting seeds, see Chapter 11. In these modules, be aware the flowers from seeds you save and sow may not look like the flowers on the plant you collected them from. Cross-pollination with other flowers is extremely likely – you may end up with a fantastic new flower, but more likely you'll end up with an inferior plant. This is especially true of seeds from F1 hybrid plants – plants that have been engineered to have particular traits such as larger flowers or a particular colour – and it is not worth collecting seeds from these plants.

Module 25 Annual cut flowers

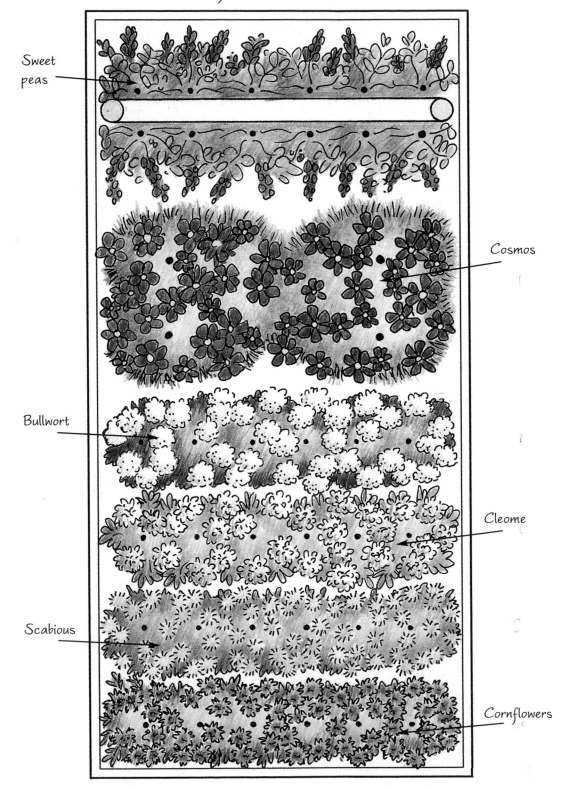

Sweet peas

Cosmos

Bullwort

Cleome

Scabious

Cornflowers

Module 25 ANNUAL CUT FLOWERS

Easy-to-grow, traditional cottage garden cut flowers that are less common in the shops. All these annuals are cut-and-come-again, providing very British posies all summer.

Bed type: annuals

Plant name	Number needed	Growth habit
Sweet peas (*Lathyrus odoratus*)	Seed: 1 packet or 12 plants	Bushy annual climber
Cosmos (*Cosmos bipinnatus*)	Seed: 1 packet or 4 plants	Tall bushy annual
Bullwort (*Ammi majus*)	Seed: 1 packet	Medium bushy annual
Cleome (*Cleome hassleriana*)	Seed: 1 packet	Medium bushy annual
Scabious (*Scabious atropurpurea*)	Seed: 1 packet	Medium bushy annual
Cornflowers (*Centaurea cyanus*)	Seed: 1 packet	Medium bushy annual

Recommended varieties, planting and maintenance information
Sweet peas
- Many different colour mixes or single types available in different scent strengths.
- Hardy annual, sow in early spring or autumn under some cover or buy plug plants. Grow up netting stretched around two posts (see p. 160).

Cosmos
- Can be bought as tall or dwarfed, single or mixed-colour seed packets. 'Purity' (white) or 'Sonata' (pink/white mix).
- Half-hardy annual, sow under cover for planting out in May/June. Taller varieties may need staking.

Bullwort
- 'Graceland' has an AGM.
- Hardy annual, station sow direct into the bed in spring. Stake and start tying in when it reaches 10–15cm tall.

Cleome
- 'Colour Mix' or 'Colour Fountain Mixed' are the best for cut flowers.
- Half-hardy annual, sow under cover from mid-January for planting out in May/June.

Scabious
- Hardy annual, sow in early spring direct or in trays to transplant.

Cornflowers
- Blue ('Blue Boy'), white, yellow, pink or burgundy/purple ('Black Ball') varieties available.
- Hardy annual, sow direct or in trays to transplant in early spring.

Module 26 Perennial cut flowers

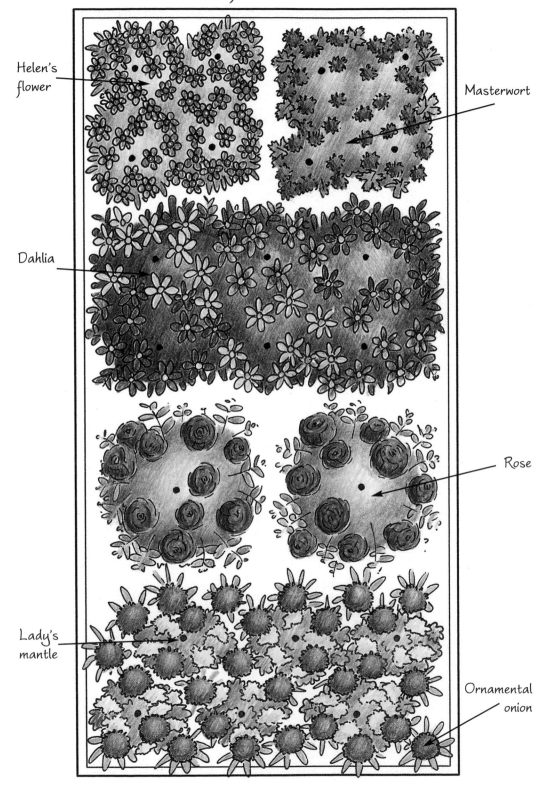

Helen's flower

Masterwort

Dahlia

Rose

Lady's mantle

Ornamental onion

Module 26 PERENNIAL CUT FLOWERS

Perennials offer a wide range of flowers over a longer season for less work than annuals. Dahlias, roses and astrantia are even cut-and-come-again.

Bed type: perennials

Plant name	Number needed	Growth habit
Helen's flower (*Helenium*)	4 plants	Medium bushy perennial
Masterwort (*Astrantia major*)	4 plants	Small bushy perennial
Dahlia (*Dahlia*)	6 plants	Medium bushy perennial
Rose (*Rosa*)	2 plants	Medium bushy shrub
Ornamental onion (*Allium*)	30 bulbs	Tall, thin bulb
Lady's mantle (*Alchemilla mollis*)	6 plants	Small bushy perennial

Recommended varieties, planting and maintenance information

Helenium
- 'Moerheim Beauty' (red/orange) is good for cutting.
- Chelsea chop (see p. 164) if desired. May need staking.

Astrantia
- The straight species is wine red or white ('Alba'), or try 'Claret' and 'Shaggy' (AGM).
- Keep cutting the flowers for it to produce more.

Dahlia
- Huge choice of flower colour and shape and foliage colour.
- Plants are frost tender, so plant out in May/June. Dig up plants (or plant in plunged pots and lift) in autumn when frost has killed the foliage and store the tubers in a dry place over winter. Or add a thick layer of mulch over the soil to protect them (this is not guaranteed, some tubers may still rot in bad winters).

Rose
- Choose a hybrid tea type. Huge choice of flower colours and scents.
- Prune to an open goblet shape of 4 stems, 4 buds from the base every (early) spring and remove the 3Ds (see p. 165).

Allium
- 'Globemaster' is especially good for cutting, but all last well.
- Plant in autumn. Remove dead foliage in mid-summer. Flowers can be left to dry on the plant for seedheads.

Alchemilla
- Cut gone-over flowers back to base for a second flush in late summer.

Module 27 Winter stems and spring bulbs

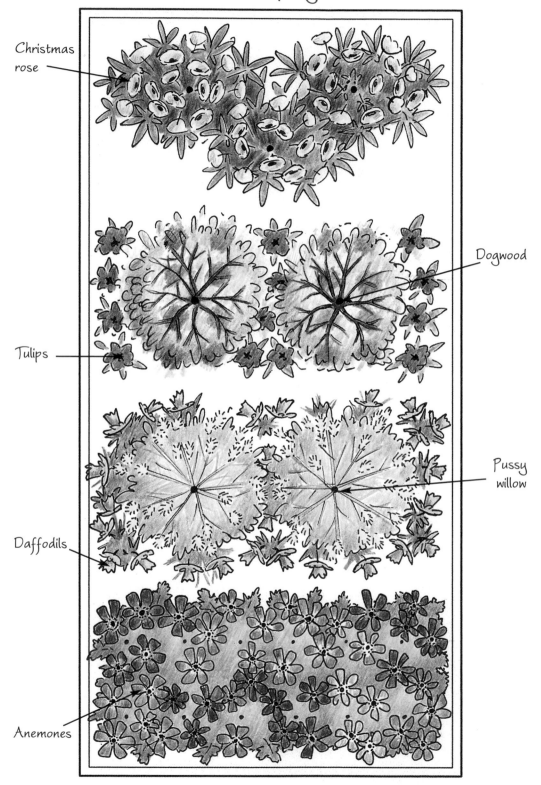

Christmas rose

Dogwood

Tulips

Pussy willow

Daffodils

Anemones

Module 27 WINTER STEMS AND SPRING BULBS

Bright red stems of dogwoods are perfect strewn with small baubles at Christmas.

Bed type: perennials

Plant name	Number needed	Growth habit
Christmas rose (*Helleborus x hybridus*)	3 plants	Small bushy perennial
Dogwoods (*Cornus alba*)	2 plants	Large bushy shrub
Tulips (*Tulipa* varieties)	40 bulbs	Medium thin bulb
Pussy willow (*Salix caprea*)	2 plants	Large bushy shrub
Daffodils (*Narcissus*)	40 bulbs	Medium thin bulb
Anemones (*Anemone coronaria*)	12 plants or 20 pips	Small bushy perennial

Recommended varieties, planting and maintenance information

Christmas rose
- Available in many colours.
- Semi-evergreen, cut off dead topgrowth in early summer as fresh leaves emerge. Remove leaves infected with fungal diseases when seen.

Dogwoods
- *Cornus alba* 'Sibirica' has crimson red stems; 'alba' types have longer, thicker stems than the spindly 'sanguinea' types.
- Cut stems two buds from the base. Remove any remaining stems in March.

Tulips
- Have all the flowers at once, or stagger early, mid- and late season varieties.
- Plant in four rows of ten bulbs beneath the dogwoods. Tidy up dead foliage – it should pull away easily.

Pussy willow
- Harvest when the catkins have just appeared; cut stems two buds from the base. Remove any remaining stems in mid-spring.

Daffodils
- Have all the flowers at once, or stagger early, mid- and late season varieties.
- Plant in four rows of ten bulbs beneath the pussy willow. Tidy away browned foliage six weeks after flowering.

Anemones
- Assorted mixes available as pips, such as 'Sweetheart Mix'.
- Plant pips about 10cm apart, potted plants as shown on the plan. Remove foliage when it has died back.

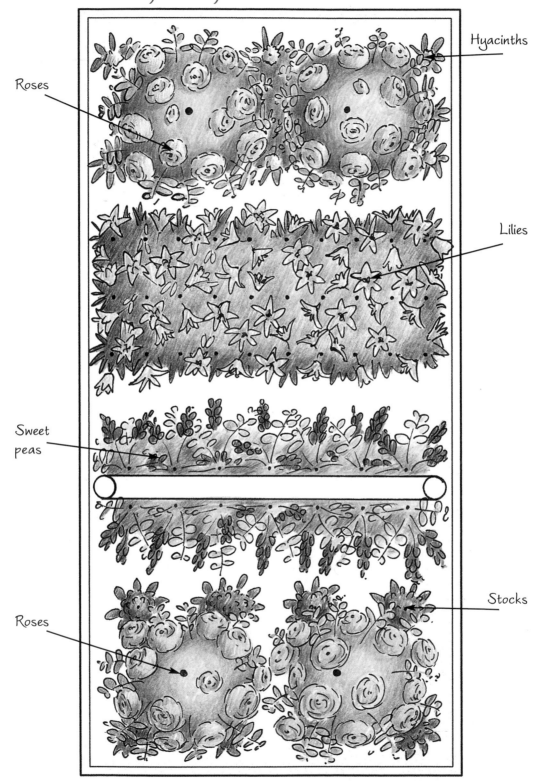

Hyacinths

Roses

Lilies

Sweet peas

Roses

Stocks

Module 28 CUT FLOWERS FOR SCENT

Many cut flowers in the shops have been bred for longevity or flower colour and their scent has been lost – especially roses. Grow your own for the best perfume.

Bed type: perennials and annuals

Plant name	Number needed	Growth habit
Roses (*Rosa*)	4 plants	Medium bushy shrub
Hyacinths (*Hyacinthus*)	20 bulbs	Small thin bulb
Stocks (*Matthiola incana*)	Seed: 1 packet or 8 plants	Small bushy annual
Lilies (*Lilium*)	30 bulbs	Tall thin bulb
Sweet peas (*Lathyrus odoratus*)	Seed: 1 packet or 12 plants	Medium bushy climber

Recommended varieties, planting and maintenance information
Roses
- Choose a hybrid tea type. Huge choice of flower colours and scents within that group.
- Prune to an open goblet shape of four stems, four buds from the base every (early) spring, before new growth starts in earnest. Remove the 3Ds at the same time (see p. 165).

Hyacinths
- All are fragrant – choose from white, pink, blue or purple flower colours.
- Plant two rows of ten bulbs under the roses.
- Plant in autumn. Remove foliage when it has died back.

Stocks
- Available in various colours and colour mixes, as seed or young plants.
- Hardy annual, sow in spring direct or in pots to transplant. Plant out in spring.

Lilies
- Oriental lilies are available in many flower colours. 'Stargazer' is a reliable classic.
- Plant in autumn, or early spring in cold areas. Stems may need staking with individual canes. Beware bright red lily beetles eating leaves and flowers – remove and kill if seen.

Sweet peas
- Many different single colours, colour mixes and scent strengths available.
- Hardy annual, sow in early spring or autumn under some cover or buy plug plants. Grow up netting stretched around two posts (see p. 160).

Module 29 White cut flowers

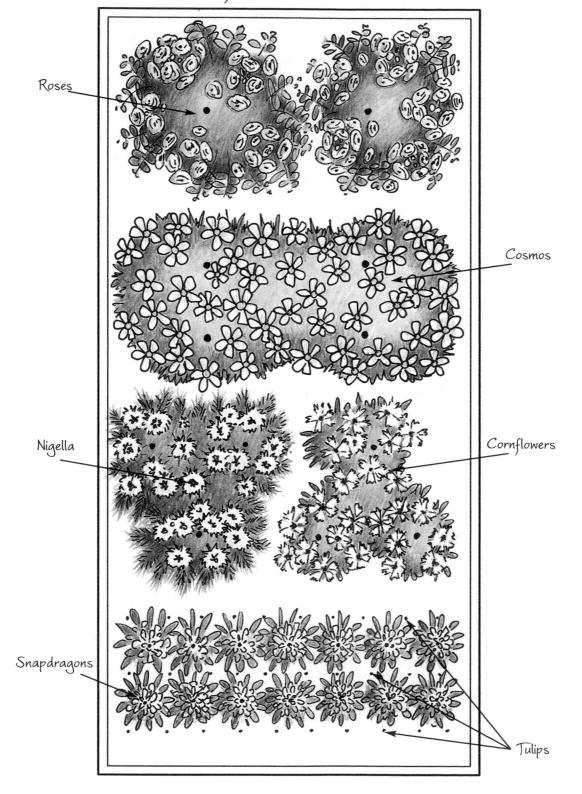

Roses

Cosmos

Nigella

Cornflowers

Snapdragons

Tulips

Module 29 **WHITE CUT FLOWERS**

The combination of white flowers and green foliage is simple but sophisticated. The striking combination of different forms in the same colour can be used to great effect on their own or combined with another cut-flower module.

Bed type: annuals and perennials

Plant name	Number needed	Growth habit
Roses (*Rosa*)	2 plants	Medium bushy shrub
Cosmos (*Cosmos bipinnatus* 'Purity')	Seed: 1 packet or 4 plants	Tall bushy annual
Nigella (*Nigella damascena* 'Miss Jekyll Alba')	Seed: 1 packet or 3 plants	Medium bushy annual
Cornflowers (*Centaurea cyanus* 'Alba')	Seed: 1 packet or 3 plants	Medium bushy annual
Snapdragons (*Antirrhinum majus*)	Seed: 1 packet or 6 plants	Medium bushy annual
Tulips (*Tulipa*)	30 bulbs	Medium thin bulb

Recommended varieties, planting and maintenance information
Roses
- Choose a hybrid tea, e.g. 'Polar Star' or 'Silver Wedding'.
- Prune to an open goblet shape of four stems, four buds from the base every (early) spring, and remove the 3Ds (see p. 165).

Cosmos
- 'Purity' is an excellent white variety.
- Half-hardy annual, sow under cover for planting out in May/June. May need staking.

Nigella
- Hardy annuals. Sow direct. Keep cutting for flowers, or leave for decorative seedheads.

Cornflowers and snapdragons
- Hardy annuals, sow direct or in pots to transplant in early spring.

Tulips
- Choose to have your bulbs flowering all at the same time, or stagger blooms with early, mid- and late season varieties. 'Maureen' is a tall-stemmed creamy-white flower.
- Tidy up browned foliage after flowering – it should pull away easily.

Chapter 9
THE MODULES: PLANTS FOR POLLINATORS AND PREDATORS

WHY WILDLIFE HELPS GARDENS AND GARDENS HELP WILDLIFE

For the fruit and vegetable beds, attracting pollinating insects is crucial. Without pollination, plants won't form seeds, or the fruit or vegetable around the seed that we want to eat. Other insects are useful in keeping our plants healthy. It is inevitable that gardens full of plants will attract bugs and other wildlife that want to eat all your hard work. You can use chemicals to minimise the damage caused by these pests, but if your garden functions as a healthy and diverse ecosystem, you should not need to. For example, aphids are a huge pest of most plants, but they are also ideal fodder for ladybirds and hoverflies. Their larvae and adults eat hundreds of aphids and other pests, while doing no harm to the plant.

A biodiverse garden is not just helpful for you as a gardener – it benefits the environment too. With the advent of large-scale agriculture and the loss of many hedgerows and other countryside habitats, back gardens are increasingly becoming wildlife havens for our threatened species. According to 'Buglife', one-third of all the food we eat depends on pollinating insects for its production, but 250 key pollinator species are currently threatened with extinction.

One problem for many insects is the long distance between food sources. Too much of our countryside, while green, is a barren wasteland for many insects. Flowers are what they need. Back gardens are becoming important 'nectar bars' – both primary food sources and useful staging posts for insects on longer journeys.

The wildlife to attract

It is true that your garden will attract many insects, both good and bad, but by planting flowers that we know are food sources for specific insects we can target the insects we want. Bees, bumblebees, hoverflies and butterflies are all pollinators. Hoverflies, ladybirds and lacewing flies are all predators of garden pests.

The basic principles of attracting pollinators and predators
Simple is best

Gardeners have not always been friends to insects; many of today's flower cultivars, bred for lots of petals, are inaccessible to bees and other insects. They can't get past the petals to the nectar source at the base of the flower. Flowers with only one set of petals (single flowers) are best. These are often the older, more traditional species rather than new varieties. For example, a single Christmas rose is preferable to a double camellia (see p. 129).

A succession of flowers through the year is more important than native flowers
To keep the insects visiting your garden over the year, you need flowers over the year. A variety of preferred nectar sources spread through the seasons is more useful to the insects than purely native plantings that only supply food for one season.

Flowers in large groups or drifts are better than small patches
Insects expend a lot of energy foraging for food. Putting the same plants in large groups or long drifts means they can move easily from flower to flower. Planting this way means the flowers are also more visible from the air to attract the insects in the first place.

Don't be too tidy
Insects, beetles, frogs and toads, hedgehogs and many other beneficial wildlife species need somewhere to hide. A clinically tidy garden is no good for them – they want piles of dry leaves that have blown up into the corner, areas of the garden that you rarely go to, pots that don't get moved regularly. In a small garden it may be difficult to balance a desire for tidiness and areas for wildlife, but leaving the edges and out-of-sight areas 'untidy' will make a big difference. However, to prevent plant diseases taking hold you will need to remove dead foliage from your module beds. If you can, keep the module beds clean and be messier around them. This should provide a good balance.

Build it and they will come
You will be surprised how quickly wildlife flocks to your garden once you start adding modules of any sort, but especially the ones in this chapter. Not included, but beneficial, is a water source. Even in the middle of the city these can attract frogs and toads (brilliant slug-eaters) and other insects and birds that can help control garden pests. Organisations such as the RHS, county Wildlife Trusts and the Royal Society for the Protection of Birds (RSPB) provide advice on making ponds.

CULTIVATION

Soil preparation
Prepare the soil as normal (see Chapter 4, p. 39).

Planting layout
Although set out in a grid like all the other modules, this chapter is where you can most easily be a bit more creative. These beds, once planted, will not be harvested so they are essentially flower borders. If you're confident you can distinguish your plants outside the grid system (labelling helps) then plant them however takes your fancy. Make sure you still adhere to the principles above, and take into account the plants' ultimate heights.

A single flower (Christmas Rose)

A double flower (Camellia)

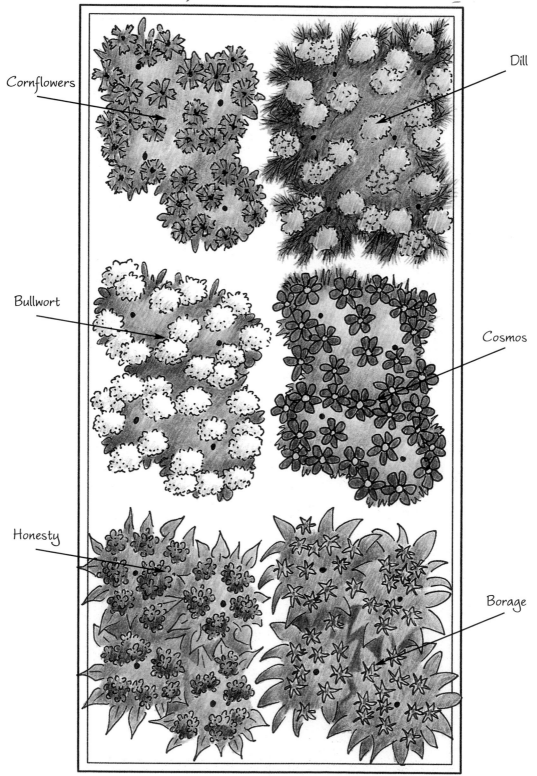

Cornflowers

Dill

Bullwort

Cosmos

Honesty

Borage

Module 30 ANNUALS FOR POLLINATORS AND PREDATORS

This module is the cheapest of the pollinators and predators modules, requires commitment for only a year, and gives the most immediate return, providing more flowers than a perennial bed would in its first year. The module contains plants for both pollinators and predators in the summer, and you will be surprised at how many insects they can attract.

Bed type: annuals

Plant name	Number needed	Growth habit
Cornflowers (*Centaurea cyanus*)	Seed: 1 packet	Medium bushy annual
Dill (*Anethum graveolens*)	Seed: 1 packet	Small bushy annual
Bullwort (*Ammi majus*)	Seed: 1 packet	Medium bushy annual
Cosmos (*Cosmos bipinnatus*)	Seed: 1 packet	Large bushy annual
Honesty (*Lunaria annua*)	Seed: 1 packet	Medium bushy annual
Borage (*Borago officinalis*)	Seed: 1 packet	Large bushy annual

Recommended varieties, planting and maintenance information
Cornflowers
- Hardy annual, sow direct or in pots to transplant in early spring.

Dill
- Hardy annual, sow direct or in pots to transplant in early spring.

Bullwort
- 'Graceland' has an AGM.
- Hardy annual, station sow direct into the bed in spring. Stake and start tying in when it reaches 10–15cm tall.

Cosmos
- Can be bought as single-colour or mixed-colour seed packets. Dwarf varieties also available.
- Half-hardy annual, sow under cover for planting out in May/June. Some of the taller varieties may need staking.

Honesty
- Hardy annual, sow direct. Will seed freely around the garden so remove seedheads if you don't want this to happen.

Borage
- Hardy annual, sow direct or in pots to transplant in early spring.

Module 31 Perennials for pollinators and predators

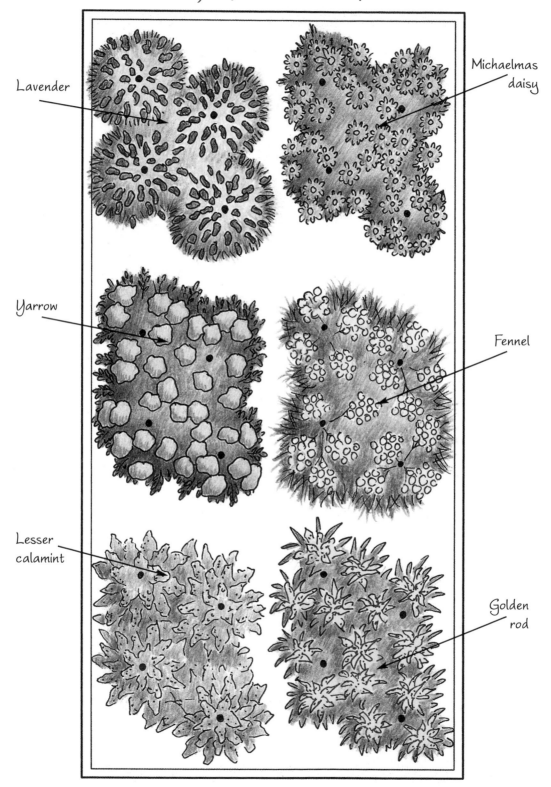

Lavender

Michaelmas daisy

Yarrow

Fennel

Lesser calamint

Golden rod

Module 31 PERENNIALS FOR POLLINATORS AND PREDATORS

This module is directed at attracting both pollinators and predators, but as it consists of herbaceous perennials is very low maintenance once planted. By including some herbs – lavender and fennel – and late summer flowering plants to keep a continuous supply of nectar and colour, it will go a long way to helping insects in your garden.

Bed type: perennials

Plant name	Number needed	Growth habit
Lavender (*Lavandula angustifolia*)	4 plants	Medium bushy evergreen shrub
Michaelmas daisy (*Aster novii-belgii*)	4 plants	Medium bushy perennial
Yarrow (*Achillea filipendula*)	4 plants	Tall bushy perennial
Fennel (*Foeniculum vulgare*)	4 plants	Tall bushy perennial
Lesser calamint (*Calamintha nepeta* subsp. *nepeta*)	4 plants	Small bushy perennial
Golden rod (*Solidago* 'Goldenmosa')	4 plants	Medium bushy perennial

Recommended varieties, planting and maintenance information
Lavender
- English lavender, *Lavandula angustifolia*, is best, but all varieties of it are also suitable. Avoid French lavender, *Lavandula stoechas*; it has fewer flowers and is less hardy.
- Clip back when the flowers have gone over, cutting to just above the lowest leaf on the new, green growth. Don't cut into the brown woody growth below.

Michaelmas daisy
- The *novii-belgii* types are smaller. Varieties with different flower colours are available within this group.
- Can be Chelsea chopped (see p. 164). Cut back dead stems in winter or early spring to ground level.

Yarrow
- Yellow or red flower colours are available.
- Cut back dead stems in winter or early spring to ground level. May need staking.

Fennel
- Green or bronze fennel could be used here, but you only use green in the kitchen.
- Treat as yarrow.

Lesser calamint and golden rod
- Cut back dead stems in winter or early spring to ground level.

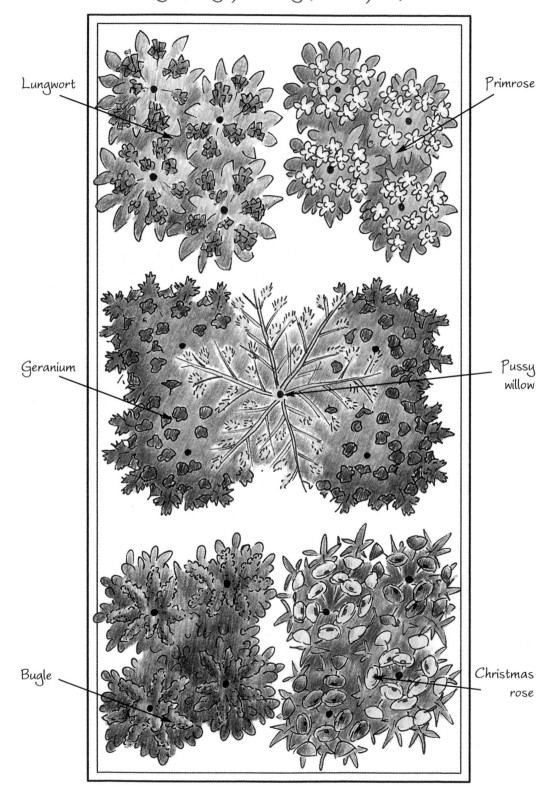

Lungwort

Primrose

Geranium

Pussy willow

Bugle

Christmas rose

Module 32 EARLY SPRING-FLOWERING PLANTS FOR POLLINATORS

Early spring is a crucial time for insects emerging from their winter hideaways. They need to find sources of food without expending a lot of energy travelling between those sources. This module provides nectar for bees and other pollinators, and some welcome early spring colour for the garden too.

Bed type: shrubs and perennials

Plant name	Number needed	Growth habit
Lungwort (*Pulmonaria officinalis*)	4 plants	Small bushy perennial
Primrose (*Primula vulgaris*)	4 plants	Small bushy perennial
Pussy willow (*Salix caprea*)	1 plant	Tall woody shrub
Geranium (*Geranium phaeum*)	4 plants	Small bushy perennial
Bugle (*Ajuga reptans*)	4 plants	Small bushy perennial
Christmas rose (*Helleborus* x *hybridus*)	4 plants	Small bushy perennial

Recommended varieties, planting and maintenance information
Lungwort, primrose and bugle
- Cut off dead flower stalks and dead leaves to the base as required – they are semi-evergreen and need very little attention. Wait until the seeds have dispersed before cutting off the flower stalks if you want the plants to spread.

Pussy willow
- The aim is to create a shape like a wine glass – a single stem (the 'leg') of about 30–50cm long that then breaks into a number of branches. Cut back the stems on top of the leg to a bud, after the catkins have gone over, before the leaves emerge.

Geranium
- Cut back the dead foliage in autumn. Cutting back all the foliage just after it has finished flowering creates a second flush of foliage and flowers later in the summer.

Christmas rose
- Available in many colours – any are good here.
- Semi-evergreen, cut off dead topgrowth in early summer when fresh leaves emerge. Leaves may get infected with fungal diseases through the year – just cut them off.

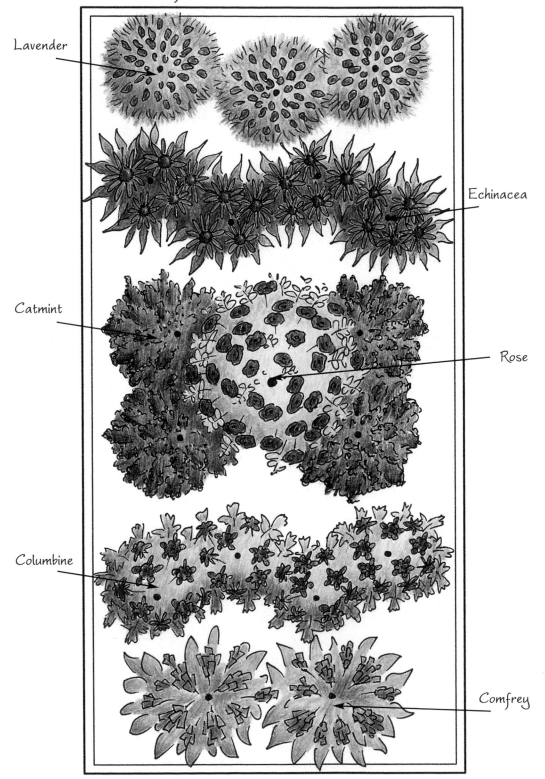

Lavender

Echinacea

Catmint

Rose

Columbine

Comfrey

Module 33 **PLANTS FOR BEES**

A perennial bed full of purple plants that bees will love all summer.

Bed type: perennials

Plant name	Number needed	Growth type
Lavender (*Lavandula angustifolia*)	3 plants	Medium bushy shrub
Echinacea (*Echinacea purpurea*)	4 plants	Medium bushy perennial
Catmint (*Nepeta*)	4 plants	Medium bushy perennial
Rose (*Rosa rugosa*)	1 plant	Large bushy shrub
Columbine (*Aquilegia vulgaris*)	4 plants	Medium bushy perennial
Comfrey (*Symphytum*)	2 plants	Medium bushy perennial

Recommended varieties, planting and maintenance information
Lavender
- English lavender, *Lavandula angustifolia*, is best, but all varieties of it are also suitable. Avoid French lavender, *Lavandula stoechas*; it has fewer flowers and is less hardy.
- Cut back in late summer to just above where the stems change from soft to woody.

Echinacea
- Don't cut back dead foliage until February/March – birds enjoy the seedheads over winter.

Catmint
- *Nepeta* 'Six Hills Giant' is reliable, will fill the space quickly and cascade over the bed edges. For more compact growth, try *Nepeta* 'Walker's Low'.
- Cut back by half after flowering to encourage a second flush of flowers.

Rose
- Pink *Rosa rugosa* (AGM) (or white 'Alba' AGM) has simple, open flowers, a great scent, and large hips for the birds in autumn.
- Prune to remove the 3Ds (see p. 165) and one or two stems to the ground each year; remove the top 10cm back to a bud in late winter/early spring.

Columbine
- Will self-seed freely unless old flower stalks are removed.

Comfrey
- *Symphytum* 'Bocking 14' is sterile, and only available as young plants. Bees like all comfries but others can be invasive.
- Cut back dead foliage in autumn/winter.

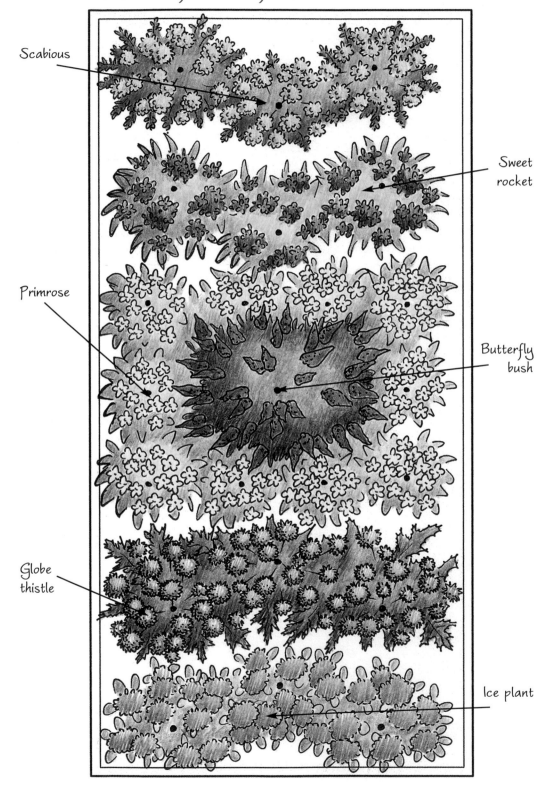

Scabious

Sweet rocket

Primrose

Butterfly bush

Globe thistle

Ice plant

Module 34 PLANTS FOR BUTTERFLIES

Butterflies are becomingly increasingly scarce so plant foods to attract them. The flip side of beautiful butterflies flitting about your flowers is their hungry caterpillars, but it's a small price to pay, especially if you're prepared for it.

Bed type: perennials

Plant name	Number needed	Growth type
Scabious (*Scabiosa columbaria*)	3 plants	Medium bushy perennial
Sweet rocket (*Hesperis matronalis*)	3 plants	Medium bushy perennial
Butterfly bush (*Buddleja davidii*)	1 plant	Tall bushy shrub
Primrose (*Primula vulgaris*)	10 plants	Small bushy perennial
Globe thistle (*Echinops sphaerocephalus*)	3 plants	Medium bushy perennial
Ice plant (*Sedum spectabile*)	3 plants	Medium bushy perennial

Recommended varieties, planting and maintenance information
Scabious
- Get *Scabiosa columbaria* (also known as *Scabiosa banatica*), a UK native.
- Plant in spring or autumn. Deadhead regularly to encourage more flowers. Cut back dead stems in autumn or winter.

Sweet rocket
- Buy as small plants or sow seeds in spring. It will need replacing every two to three years. The flower colour varies within the species from white to purple.
- Cut back dead stems in autumn/winter.

Butterfly bush
- Varieties in the *B. davidii* group would also be fine.
- Prune in March, cutting back stems to two or three buds above last year's cuts, cutting to just above a rosette of new leaves. Deadhead in autumn to prevent it seeding about the garden.

Primrose
- Remove old flower stems and dead leaves as they are liable to rotting.

Globe thistle
- Leave the seedheads over winter and cut back all stems to the ground in February.

Ice plant
- If not Chelsea chopped (see p. 164) it may need staking.
- Cut back dead stems in winter.

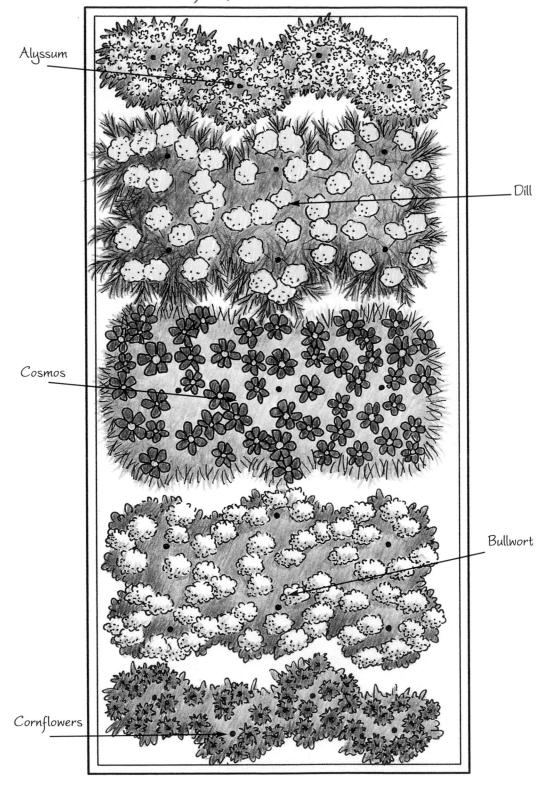

Alyssum

Dill

Cosmos

Bullwort

Cornflowers

Module 35 ANNUALS FOR PREDATORS

The types of insects that will come and feast on your garden pests are attracted to different flower types to those that bees and butterflies prefer. This bed of annuals is attractive to look at and will also appeal to hoverflies and ladybirds.

Bed type: annuals

Plant name	Number needed	Growth type
Alyssum (*Alyssum*)	Seed: 1 packet or 4 plants	Small bushy annual
Dill (*Anethum graveolens*)	Seed: 1 packet or 6 young plants	Small thin annual
Cosmos (*Cosmos bipinnatus*)	Seed: 1 packet or 3 young plants	Tall bushy annual
Bullwort (*Ammi majus*)	Seed: 1 packet or 6 young plants	Medium bushy annual
Cornflowers (*Centaurea cyanus*)	Seed: 1 packet or 4 young plants	Medium bushy annual

Recommended varieties, planting and maintenance information
Alyssum
- *Alyssum* 'Sweet White' is a pretty variety with a good scent.
- Half-hardy annual, sow under cover and transplant in May/June or sow direct in May.

Dill
- Hardy annual, sow direct in spring.

Cosmos
- Any single-flowered varieties would suit the purpose.
- Half-hardy annual, sow under cover and transplant in May/June. Taller varieties may need staking.

Bullwort
- Hardy annual, station sow direct into the bed in spring. Stake and start tying in when it reaches 10–15cm tall.

Cornflowers
- Blue ('Blue Boy'), white, yellow, pink or burgundy/purple ('Black Ball') varieties available.
- Hardy annual, sow direct or in pots to transplant in early spring.

Module 36 Perennials for predators

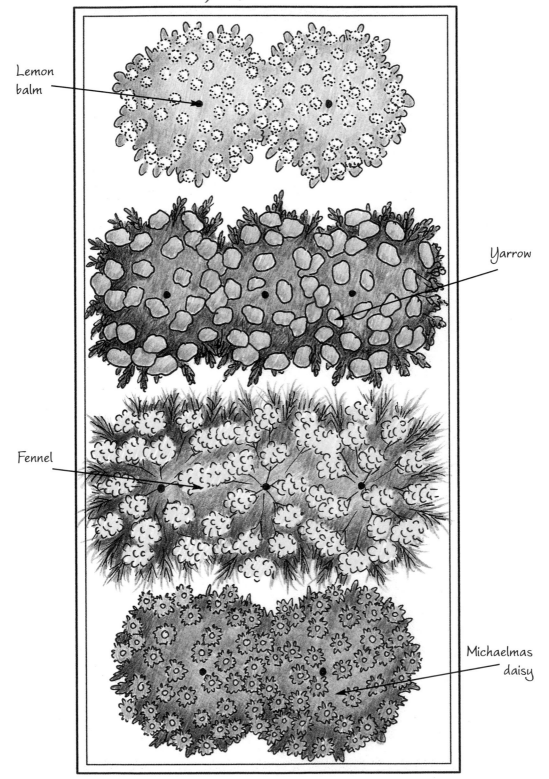

Lemon balm

Yarrow

Fennel

Michaelmas daisy

Module 36 PERENNIALS FOR PREDATORS

This bed contains fewer varieties of plants than the Annuals for Predators module, but the larger swathes of flowers will be just as attractive to beneficial insects. It contains taller plants, so would be a good one to site along a fence or at the back of the garden, and will be interesting to look at all summer.

Bed type: perennials

Plant name	Number needed	Growth type
Lemon balm (*Melissa officinalis*)	2 plants	Medium bushy perennial
Yarrow (*Achillea filipendula*)	3 plants	Medium bushy perennial
Fennel (*Foeniculum vulgare*)	3 plants	Tall bushy perennial
Michaelmas daisy (*Aster amellus*)	2 plants	Medium bushy perennial

Recommended varieties, planting and maintenance information
Lemon balm
● Plant in spring or autumn. Cut back the dead stems to the ground in autumn.

Yarrow
● Any of the yellow- or red-flowering varieties would be suitable.
● Plant in spring or autumn. Taller varieties may need staking. Cut back the dead stems to the ground in late winter – the seedheads are attractive over winter.

Fennel
● The ordinary green *Foeniculum vulgare* is best, but bronze fennel will also do.
● Plant in spring or autumn. Should only need staking in windy conditions. Cut back the dead stems to the ground in autumn – before the plant has a chance to drop its seeds if you don't want it to spread.

Michaelmas daisy
● *Aster amellus* varieties would be most suited to this purpose, but any *Aster* would do.
● Plant in spring or autumn. Can be Chelsea chopped (see p. 164), may need staking otherwise. Cut back the dead stems to the ground in autumn – they are not attractive over winter.

Chapter 10
THE MODULES: GROW YOUR OWN GARDEN SUPPLIES

WHY IT'S GOOD TO GROW YOUR OWN GARDEN SUPPLIES

If you have the space, grow your own stakes and fertiliser. A sustainably coppiced hazel bush can keep you supplied with both long canes and smaller twiggy bits to support peas and chillies or weave into a wigwam. It will be a habitat for wildlife, and perhaps even provide a few hazelnuts. Hazel poles are much more attractive than bamboo canes, which have probably been imported across the world to get to your garden centre, and have a rougher surface to help the plants climbing up them.

Shop-bought fertilisers are a waste of money if you have room to grow your own comfrey. Many non-organic liquid feeds are expensive, and synthetically produced in factories (often based on petro-chemicals). Organic options are available, such as seaweed-based liquid feeds, but are generally imported.

Far better then to use comfrey growing yards from your own crops. Trials have shown that comfrey has far higher levels of nutrients than manure and most synthetic fertilisers. Plus it's free, and will happily grow in that shady patch of your garden. The best performer, Comfrey 'Bocking 14', is sterile, so won't seed all over your garden like other comfreys.

CULTIVATION

Soil preparation
Prepare the soil as normal (see Chapter 4, p. 39).

Planting times and pot sizes
The larger the hazel you buy, the sooner you will be able to cut enough canes to use in the garden, although it is a fast-growing plant. If you can afford a larger pot, a 10 or 15 litre size would be ideal (the plant should be at least 6 feet tall).

Plant the hazel in autumn or spring, and the comfrey in spring (if you're buying small plants of 'Bocking 14' this is when they will be available).

USING COMFREY AS A FERTILISER

It's better to take a few leaves from each plant than every leaf from one plant. This won't stress the plant, which will have enough energy to keep growing and expanding.

The easiest way to use comfrey is to chop the leaves roughly and spread them around the base of your veg or fruit. The leaves act as a mulch and, as they break down, release their nutrients into the soil.

There are two ways to make a liquid feed. The easiest is to add a handful of fresh leaves to a bucket of water, cover and leave it to steep for a week. Then remove the leaves and use the resulting 'tea' to water your plants. The only problem is the leaves are breaking down anaerobically, and this process produces very smelly gases.

The better method involves a bit of DIY. The aim is to collect the juices of the comfrey leaves as they rot down, and then dilute this concentrate. Two buckets (one small enough to fit inside the other), a board cut to fit flat inside the base of the inner bucket and a heavy weight is all you need, but rig up something fancier if you prefer. Drill some holes in the bottom of the inner bucket, and put it inside the other. Space it off the bottom with a brick or upturned flower pot it necessary. Put the leaves in the inner bucket, with the board and weight on top (see photo, p. 147). Leave them to rot down and drip into the bucket below, replacing the leaves every few weeks. Dilute the concentrated juice at a minimum of 15:1.

Use the tea to water your plants once or twice a week, watering the foliage as well (the nutrients can also be absorbed by the leaves), but don't use it for two weeks before harvesting. It's ideal for fruit and vegetables, but all your plants will benefit from it.

Finally, you can also add comfrey leaves to your compost heap. The nutrients will be in the resulting compost, and they are an activator, helping to speed up the rotting process.

USING HAZEL FOR GARDEN STAKES

Hazel is coppiced in two ways. Either all of its stems are cut off to the base and it grows back over a number of years (as one of many plants cut in rotation), or only a few stems are cut every year. In a garden context, the latter is the best method, but if your plant gets out of hand, you can always chop it all down and start again.

Use a pruning saw or loppers to cut the oldest stems (the thickest and tallest) close to the ground. Cutting the stem slightly higher first and then cutting off the stub to the ground will prevent the bark tearing or a ragged cut. Take out a third of the oldest stems every year; this will give a good supply of poles for wigwams and rejuvenate the shrub to keep it tidy.

If you need clean poles, cut off the side branches and reserve them to use as supports for smaller plants. If you are using them for bean poles, keep the side branches on and wind them into your wigwam sideways – the plants will appreciate the extra support. Cutting the base of your pole into a point helps drive it into the ground.

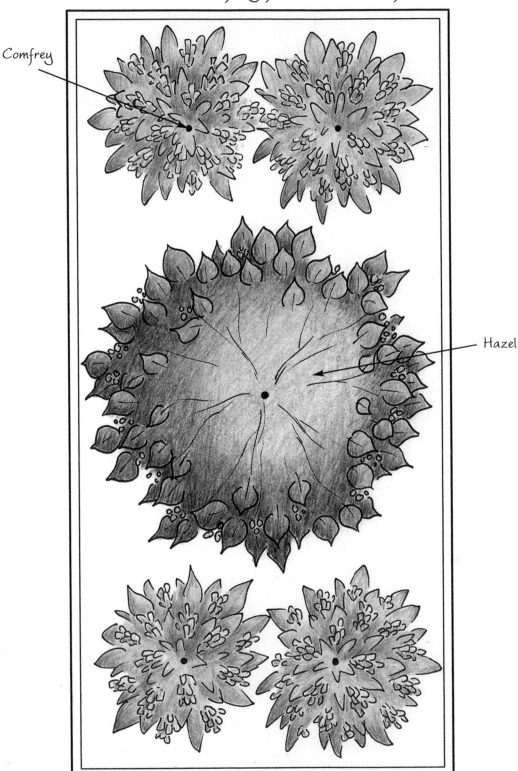

Comfrey

Hazel

Module 37 HAZEL AND COMFREY FOR STAKES AND FERTILISER

This module, plus a healthy compost heap, can make your garden more or less self-sufficient. It is very low maintenance, and will grow happily at the end of the garden in a shady, out-of-the-way spot, or use it for a low-maintenance but very useful front garden. Bees will also appreciate the comfrey flowers.

Bed type: perennials and shrub

Plant name	Number needed	Growth habit
Hazel (*Corylus avellana*)	1 plant	Large deciduous shrub
Comfrey (*Symphytum* 'Bocking 14')	4 plants	Medium bushy perennial

Recommended varieties, planting and maintenance information
Hazel
- There are varieties available of hazel, some with purple leaves, but the native species is best for this situation as it is an appropriate size.
- Coppice every year (see p. 146).

Comfrey
- Some varieties of comfrey seed freely all over the garden, and once established are difficult to weed out. Sterile 'Bocking 14' is only available to buy as small plants.
- Cut leaves as required to make fertiliser.

Chapter 11
GENERAL MAINTENANCE

TOOLS AND EQUIPMENT

Although the racks of tools in the garden centres would suggest that you need a small warehouse just to store them, you don't need much to get started as a gardener. Below is a list of the basic equipment you'll need. This needn't be prohibitively expensive – secondhand, but perfectly serviceable, tools can be found at boot fairs, or share with neighbours or other allotment-holders. As with many things, the more you spend the better quality your tools are likely to be, so the list also includes details of things to look for. If you can't afford to splash out straight away, get cheaper versions and invest in better tools as you continue to garden. Reliable brands are Bulldog, Wolf and Felco (for secateurs and saws).

Essential tools

- A *spade*. Look for a strong join between the spade and the handle. Available in full or narrower border (sometimes called ladies!) widths - using the latter will take longer but be kinder on your back as you're not lifting as much weight each time.
- A *hand fork*. A comfortable handle is crucial - you may prefer the long-handled versions, which allow you to reach more easily, but the normal short handles give more control.
- A *trowel*. As for hand forks. For planting out plugs and potted plants.
- A *pair of secateurs*. Worth investing in a decent pair if you can – Felco are the best brand, and they offer servicing (for a fee). Bypass blades (where the blades work like a pair of scissors) are better than the anvil style (where one blade hits on to a flat surface).
- A *rake*. For levelling the soil after digging, so go for strong tines not the springy wire ones used to rake up leaves. The width is up to you; a wide rake is better for levelling empty beds, but a narrow one can level the bed and be used to tidy up the soil after weeding between rows too.
- A *watering can*. Get one with a capacity of around 10l – more and it'll be too heavy, less and you have to do more trips to the tap. Make sure it has a rose attachment for the end of the spout.
- *Garden string*. Soft green garden string is better than standard white string as it's kinder on the plant stems.

Useful but not essential tools

- A *large or border fork*. Useful for turning compost into the soil, breaking up clods of soil and digging up potatoes. Look for the same qualities as spades.

- *A wheelbarrow.* Make sure you can pump up, or replace, the wheel easily. Builders' barrows are often a better choice than garden barrows.
- *A hoe.* For scraping off small annual weeds (which are left to dry and die). Quick weeding, but can disturb the plants' roots and soil structure.
- *A pruning saw or loppers.* For cutting larger branches such as hazel stems.

Tool care

Keep your tools in good condition to prolong their life. Keep them clean to help prevent any plant diseases spreading. Use a brush to clean off mud (avoid washing them in water to prevent rusting), and oil your secateurs regularly. Sharpen blades with a file or a specialist sharpening tool/stone.

WATERING

Most plants will survive dry spells without additional watering, but are less likely to produce a decent crop. Leafy annual plants (lettuce, spinach, etc.) are more likely to bolt in dry conditions and fruiting plants may produce very small fruit/veg or nothing at all. It is therefore important that your plants always have an adequate supply of water, but water smart.

Check if the soil needs watering

It may be dry and crusty on the surface after a sunny day but still have plenty of moisture in the soil, or look wet after a shower but be dry as dust beneath. The best way to check is the most basic – stick your finger in it! The soil should be moist but not wet. Don't worry about it unduly – plants can survive a lot before they wilt or drown beyond retrieval – you will get a feel for it the longer you garden.

Water efficiently

If you do need to water, do so efficiently. Give the beds a good thorough soaking in the early morning or evening, directing a gentle flow (to avoid soil erosion) to the soil beneath the plants, not over the leaves. Unless you are applying foliar feed or comfrey tea, splashing a bit of water over the top will do more harm than good. The water will only penetrate the topmost layer of soil, encouraging the roots to stay near the surface where they will dry out faster, and the humidity from the evaporation will encourage fungal diseases. Aim for ten litres per square metre, i.e. a large watering can for half a module.

Bottom line
| |
Water thoroughly when the soil needs it and you can't go far wrong. Some plants need watering more than others, but regular checking will prevent any catastrophes.

FEEDING YOUR PLANTS

Well-prepared soil with plenty of organic matter and perhaps some controlled-release fertiliser will go a long way to providing the nutrients your plants need to grow and crop well, but you can give them extra help with more fertiliser/food. The main elements that may need a boost are nitrogen and potassium. Nitrogen is needed for green, leafy growth, potassium helps the plant produce fruit. Phosphorus (which helps root growth) is also usually included in fertilisers.

Beware over-feeding your plants. Too much fertiliser can become toxic, and too much nitrogen will promote lots of fresh, sappy growth, which is heaven for aphids and other pests. Follow the instructions on the packet for the correct dosage.

Buying fertilisers

Fertilisers are available that have more of one nutrient than the others, depending on what you are applying it to. For example, you would give lettuce more nitrogen and tomatoes more potassium. The ratio of nutrients is shown on the label of the product as the NPK content, where N is for nitrogen, P for phosphorus, and K for potassium (its official chemical name is kalium).

Most all-purpose vegetable fertilisers will suit all your modules, but for fruit and cut flowers, a high-potassium feed (generally sold as tomato feed) would be better. Liquid fertilisers will give faster results than granular, and are best applied to boost a plant as it starts to fruit.

The alternative is to make your own. Follow the instructions in Chapter 10 (p. 145) for making comfrey fertiliser. You can use nettles instead if you don't have space for the module.

───────────── **Bottom line** ─────────────

Adding an all-purpose or home-made liquid feed to the watering can once a week should keep your plants healthy and cropping well.

WEEDING: IDENTIFYING AND REMOVING WEEDS

Your garden, no matter how well you look after it, will get weeds. There is no escape. Seeds will be blown in on the wind, be dropped by birds or be brought to the surface by cultivation, having lain dormant for many years. Weeding can cause a crisis of confidence in the beginner gardener, with weeds being left to get too big because you're not sure what they are, but removing them is so important.

Weeds are plants growing where you don't want them to. Most are native wildflowers or have self-sown from plants you have deliberately put elsewhere. Some, such as nettles, sheep's sorrel and dandelions, are edible. They play host to a diverse range of wildlife that can benefit your garden, but their potential damage outweighs their benefits.

Why weeding is important

The main reason for removing weeds is to remove the competition for your plants. Weeds are pioneers, the first to colonise bare soil and fast growing. They compete with your plants for water, nutrients and light, and can smother even established plants within a season. Just look at how big they can get in such a short time; all that water, light and nutrition could have been feeding your plants instead. Weeds also provide habitats for pests, especially slugs and snails that like somewhere shady and damp, and can be overwintering hosts for plant diseases.

How to remove weeds

So, weeds should be got rid of, but don't panic. The size and layout of the modules in this book have been designed to make it easy. If you weed a couple of rows every time you go out to harvest, you should be able to keep on top of the weeds without having to put aside your weekend to 'do the garden'. Labelling rows helps, and many seed packets now also have a picture of the plant as a seedling to help identify it.

If you never let the weeds get too big, then it should not be a problem to remove them simply by pulling them up by hand. However, if your weeds have got a bit out of hand (and it happens), it's best to use a hand fork to get all the root out and to avoid disturbing the plants around them too much.

It is especially important to use a hand fork for larger perennial weeds. Perennial weeds use their roots to regenerate (even from the smallest fragment), so you must get all of the root out. It will be either a tap root, like dandelions, or creeping rhizomes, like couch grass (see p. 155 for illustrations of root types).

The danger in letting annual weeds get too big is when they flower and set seed. If you consider that each annual weed has the ability to produce hundreds if not thousands of seeds, all of which may potentially germinate in your garden, it motivates you to remove them before they do so. The adage 'one year's seeding, seven years' weeding' is probably, depressingly, an understatement.

Weeding between your established plants, it is not advisable to use weedkiller sprays as there is always the risk that there will be some drift or splash onto your carefully raised plants. Weedkillers are best reserved for spraying large areas.

Identifying weeds

On the following pages are the most common garden weeds. Every garden tends to have a problem weed, generally a perennial, and this tends to be something you learn to tolerate at a low level. Weeds coming from a neighbour's garden are less easy to endure.

Bottom line

Follow the module layout and it should be easy to identify the weeds. A few minutes' weeding every day is best for your plants and your morale.

Name	Appearance	Description
Dandelion (*Taraxacum officinale*)		Perennial, but also seeds freely. Long tap root.
Couch grass (*Elymus repens*)	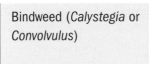 	Perennial, white fleshy roots running horizontally through the soil.
Bindweed (*Calystegia* or *Convolvulus*)		Perennial, white fleshy roots run under the surface and deep into the ground. Topgrowth twines over other plants to climb upwards.

Name	Appearance	Description
Stinging nettle (*Urtica dioica*)		Perennial, yellow roots.
Annual nettle (*Urtica urens*)		Annual, smaller and with fibrous roots that don't spread like the perennial nettle.
Dock (*Rumex obtusifolius*)		Perennial, also seeds freely. Deep, orange-yellow tap root.

Name	Appearance	Description
Ground elder (*Aegopodium podagraria*)		Perennial, especially pernicious. Spreads and regenerates quickly from white, fleshy roots. Continually removing topgrowth and as much root as possible will weaken it eventually.
Grass (*Poa annua*)		Annual, flowers and seeds quickly.
Chickweed (*Stellaria media*)		Annual, forms a large mat of small stems and leaves.

Name	Appearance	Description
Speedwell (*Veronica*)		Annual, forms a large mat of small stems and leaves.
Groundsel (*Senecio vulgaris*)		Annual, can flower when small or large depending on conditions.
Thistles (various types)		Annuals and perennials. Some have large tap roots, all seed freely.

Name	Appearance	Description
Plantain (*Plantago major*)		Herbaceous perennial, but also seeds freely. Fibrous roots. Some species have broad, round leaves, others have narrower, longer leaves, but all are ridged.
Hairy bittercress (*Cardamine hirsuta*)		Annual or ephemeral. Can flower on hardly any leaf growth. Seed pods explode when touched, spreading seeds.
Sheep's sorrel (*Rumex acetosella*)		Perennial, spreading roots. Leaf shape said to look like a sheep's head. Indicative of acidic soil.

Name	Appearance	Description
Creeping buttercup (*Ranunculus repens*)	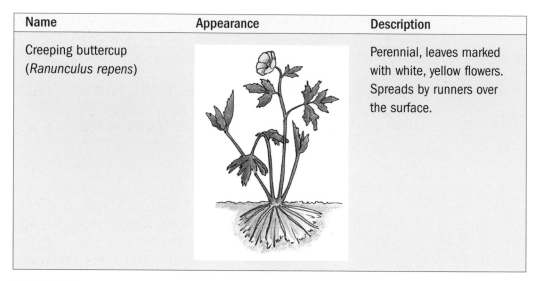	Perennial, leaves marked with white, yellow flowers. Spreads by runners over the surface.

STAKING

Some plants need extra support to prevent them from falling over under their own weight, especially if your garden is exposed. The best method depends on the plant type.

Staking tall vegetables, herbs and herbaceous perennials

These are plants that will, generally, hold themselves upright, but if they get buffeted by winds their stems may break, for example (chilli) peppers, angelica, fennel and dahlias. Some support in a couple of places up the stems should be sufficient.

If you want to buy purpose-made supports, go for the metal hoops (preferably the ones with a grid over the top) that the plants can grow up through. Choose a height appropriate for the plant. All you need to do is put them in place in the spring before the plant starts growing in earnest, and tuck in any wayward stems.

Alternatively, a hazel or bamboo cane and some string does a perfectly good job. Drive the cane into the ground to a good depth so that it stands securely and doesn't wobble at the base. Do this as close as possible to the centre of the plant. You need about 1m above ground. Tie in the stems, not too tightly, to the cane using green garden string (it's softer and better camouflaged). Tie in the stems a couple of times, or as needed, with the first tie at about 50cm high. If the plant has a lot of stems, tie them to the cane in groups rather than one large bunch.

Providing support for climbing plants

Peas, sweet peas and climbing beans all need something to grow up. Climbing beans will happily twine themselves around a single cane, but sweet peas and peas need more to hold on to, so bear this in mind if you prefer buying metal obelisks rather than making your own.

To make a wigwam of canes for your climbing beans, take six hazel or bamboo canes about 2.5m long (50cm will be in the ground and you will still be able to reach the top). Space them equally in a circle shape and push in securely. Tie together at the very top.

For sweet peas, the modules use pea and bean netting (netting with large square apertures) stretched all the way round two posts, so the sweet peas can grow up either side. The posts should have about 1.5m above ground and be large enough to give a gap between the netting on either side.

Making a hazel or willow wigwam

Woven willow wigwams are attractive supports for sweet peas, home-made or bought. If you don't have a cheap or free source of willow or hazel stems (such as from Module 37), it may be more economical to purchase one ready-made. An obelisk made of natural materials should last two to three years if it is stored in a garage or shed when not in use.

Peas and sweet peas do not grow as tall as climbing beans, so allow 1.5m above ground, 50cm below. Construct the base as you would for climbing beans above. Then take thinner, pliable stems of willow or hazel and weave them between the upright canes.

The only rule is not to start the winding stems in the same place each time – they should follow on from each other around the uprights. Otherwise, how you make the wigwam is up to you. You do not need to make it solid, but avoid gaps of more than 10cm. Spiralling a line of woven stems up and around the base canes is an easy and attractive option.

Providing support for single-stem plants

Plants such as sunflowers and tomatoes bear heavy flowers and fruit on a thick single stem that nonetheless needs support to keep it upright. The canes used for these plants need to be substantial to avoid breaking, and driven well into the ground to prevent leaning. Rather than use hazel or bamboo canes, unless you can find especially thick ones, it may be better to invest in cut wooden stakes from a garden centre that can be hammered in. Tie on the plant regularly using a figure-of-eight loop of garden string, tying off the ends against the stake, not the stem. Alternatively, if you prefer, purchase metal stakes and specific supports for tomatoes.

Staking fruit tree cordons

Whatever fruit you choose, each cordon needs a vertical post support. Use posts 2.5m long and drive them 60cm into the ground in place before planting. Each tree should be planted so that the prevailing wind blows the stem back onto the stake, and secured with a tree tie.

Staking fruit tree stepovers

Drive in a short stake leaving about 45cm above the ground, in the place where each tree is to be planted, 30cm in from the edge of the bed. Secure a strong, taut wire between the stakes around the bed.

Staking raspberry canes

Each row of raspberries needs two horizontal wires to be tied into. Drive 2.5m posts 60–75cm into the ground at either end of the row. You may wish to add supporting struts. Secure thick galvanised wire to the posts, the first halfway up the post and the other just below the top. Tie in the canes to both wires.

Bottom line

As long as your support holds up the plant, that is all that's needed. It's much easier to stake a plant before it needs it than to tie in heavy growth later in the season. Use your common sense to determine what needs staking.

PROTECTING YOUR CROPS

Plants sometimes need protection from the elements and from pests. There are many different types of cloches and tunnels, but very few will enhance the look of your garden, so only use protective structures over your plants when absolutely necessary.

Protection from the elements

In general, once all risk of frost has passed, no module will need protection. The foliage of first early potatoes emerges in spring and can be damaged by frost. Protect plants from frost with plastic or glass tunnels or cloches. It is also possible to buy lengths of horticultural fleece and lay them directly over potatoes in a double layer (weighing down the edges). Sheets of newspaper can also work when at least four layers thick. Those plants that will need to be brought inside over winter are specified in the individual modules.

As you become more experienced at growing, you may wish to extend the season by growing plants (such as salads and strawberries) under cover earlier or later in the year.

For Module 6, Hot Sun Veg, using plastic or glass cloches is not essential but will help you get a good crop, especially in a poor summer. Chillies, aubergines and peppers all originate from warmer climates than the UK, so a protective structure to raise the temperature around the plants will help them grow well.

Protection from pests

Soft fruit needs protecting from birds but not insects – indeed, insects are needed for pollination – so a standard netting is all that is required. Brassicas need a finer mesh to stop the cabbage white butterfly, which will lay its eggs on your plants so that its caterpillars can eat their way through your sprouts and kale. The mesh will also stop the pigeons in the winter months. Growing carrot varieties resistant to carrot fly will help, but if you want to minimise the risk, they need covering with the finest mesh or horticultural fleece, or plastic tunnels if you don't want to buy too many different types of kit.

There are many types of protective structure available, across a range of prices. Inevitably it is unlikely you will find one that meets all your needs. The easiest to use, and remove to harvest, weed or water, are the ready-made tunnels of mesh or plastic. Alternatively, buy a roll of netting and stretch it over posts, or canes bent into a hoop, pegging it down securely on all sides.

Bird-scarers

You may find bird-scarers more aesthetically pleasing than netting, but they are less efficient. Either buy them, or make your own: old CDs hung on string so they flash in the sun and bang in the wind are a cheap option. Whatever you use, move them around the garden every few days – birds will soon be contemptuous of familiar scarers.

Bottom line

A garden of netting and plastic is not pretty. The best way to deter larger pests is to be in your garden as much as possible, and most plants will still crop with no protection.

PEST AND DISEASE CONTROL

As with weeds, it is inevitable that your garden will experience some level of pest infestation or disease infection at some point. For information about a particular problem, refer to the Further Reading section but prevention is better than cure.

First, cultivate a healthy, biodiverse population of predators, i.e. insects, amphibians and mammals, that will eat the pests. Plant at least one pollinator or herb module, and avoid using pesticides (which often kill all insects, including the beneficial ones).

Be tidy and clean where appropriate. Let fallen leaves and twigs accumulate around the garden edges over winter to provide homes for beetles and other beneficial insects, and likewise leave the stems of herbaceous perennials standing until February (see p. 164). However, keep your module beds tidy. Plant diseases can survive in the fallen leaves and fruit of the crops they infect; clear out old crops once they are finished too. Keep your tools clean and sharp (ragged cuts are more prone to infection).

Rotate modules over the years (see p. 10) to prevent the build-up of soil-borne diseases, and add plenty of organic matter to cultivate a healthy soil.

Pests and diseases are much more likely to succeed if your plants are weak, so avoid stressing them by keeping them well-watered, fed and protected from frosts or other damaging weather (where necessary). Remove broken branches or shoots with a clean cut back to a bud or to the main stem.

It is much easier to deal with infection or infestation if you catch it early. It may be possible then just to remove the affected part. Frequent checking of your plants is therefore advisable. It doesn't have to be a chore – a few minutes having a close look is better than leaving it to the end of the week to do all at once. Many pests live on the underside of the leaves, or in the shoot tips among the furled leaves, so check those areas closely.

Bottom line

Keep your plants healthy and your garden biodiverse and you shouldn't suffer too much from pests or diseases. Check regularly to stop infestations and infections taking hold.

CUTTING BACK AND PRUNING

Cutting back herbaceous plants

Herbaceous perennials and bulbs produce growth that dies back until the following spring. This should be removed, but only once the plant has been able to store enough energy in its roots to re-grow next year, i.e. once the stems and leaves have browned and died.

Spring bulb growth should be removed in early summer. However, some herbaceous perennials have attractive stems and seedheads in the winter, and can be left standing until January/February, just before the new growth starts again. This also provides winter habitats for insects and other animals. Alternatively, if you want to tidy your garden for the winter, cut back stems in late autumn. Cut off all the stems to ground level, trying to avoid leaving little stumps that will look untidy as the plant begins to grow again.

The Chelsea chop

So-named because it is carried out during the week of the Chelsea Flower Show, the last week in May. This technique makes herbaceous perennials bushier, more sturdy, and less in need of staking. It also delays their flowering by a few weeks. Use it on late-summer flowering herbaceous perennials – it is specified in the modules where applicable.

Using secateurs or hedging shears, chop off the top third to a half of the foliage. It's neater to cut every stem individually above a leaf node, but it will come back fast and cover the cut either way. It looks alarmingly ugly at first, but you'll reap the benefits later in the year.

Pruning woody plants

Pruning is a word that can strike fear into the hearts of novice gardeners, but it's really not that complicated. It's how gardeners control the growth of woody shrubs and trees, keeping them to a suitable size and healthy. Most pruning is needed in the fruit and cut flower modules, each of which supply the basic methods, but see also Further Reading for books and free online advice sheets.

Whatever you are pruning, before you do anything else always take out any dead stems, anything that is broken or damaged, and anything that is diseased, cutting back to just above a healthy bud in each case. Then take out any branches crossing each other closely, and then start any remaining pruning you need to do. Taking out the dead, damaged, diseased and duplicate (crossing) is known as the 3Ds or 4Ds.

Pruning 'back to four buds' means taking off all growth above the fourth bud (leaf or pair of leaves in summer) on any lateral branches off the main stem, as shown in the photo overleaf. How many buds you prune back to depends on the plant type and time of year – check each module for specific details.

Bottom line

Cutting back is removing dead topgrowth of plants so your garden isn't full of ugly brown, rotting plant material.
Pruning is not scary. Always take off less rather than more to start with and remember it's unlikely your plants will look like the idealised ones in the textbooks.

COMPOSTING

If you are going to garden, then it's good to compost. It makes financial and environmental sense. Entire books are devoted to the 'art' of making good compost, but it comes down to a few basic principles that anyone can achieve.

Siting your compost area

Designate a space in the garden for your compost heaps or bays. You could construct a couple of basic boxes from old planks or pallets, use ready-made plastic bins (which many councils supply free or for a small charge), or have free-standing piles. A contained system is best to avoid attracting rodents, especially if you add kitchen waste to the pile.

Compost heaps are often put in the darkest, dampest corner of the garden, but the rotting material needs heat to break down efficiently, so somewhere out of sight but still in the sun is best. Consider having a screen of plants to obscure the heap from the house and the rest of the garden. Frequent noise and activity will also deter rodents.

Get a good balance in your compost heap

Many compost heaps fail because they do not have enough dry or brown matter in them, and end up as a foul-smelling sludge. Aim for a 50/50 split between green and brown to keep the heap oxygenated, so it can break down properly. Brown matter is wood, sturdy stems of perennials, paper and card, ash, fallen leaves – anything relatively dry. Green matter is weeds, crop debris, grass clippings, kitchen waste – anything fresh and with a high water content. It helps if you chop up larger bits of material that you are adding to the heap to increase their surface area for the bacteria to start breaking them down, and avoids larger stems or twigs being left in the end result. Very large branches won't rot down fast enough in the heap – leave them elsewhere for invertebrates to colonise.

Meat, fish and cooked kitchen waste cannot be composted in a regular garden heap (the temperatures do not get high enough to decompose it safely); use a wormery or bran-based composting system if the council doesn't collect it and you don't want to send this type of waste to landfill.

Turning your compost heap

Regular turning of the compost helps aerate it so that it breaks down faster. It's a good job for a cold day as the heat from the rotting process gets released as you turn it. You want to have one heap that you are turning and allowing to rot down, and another that you are adding fresh material to. When the first heap is ready to use, that space is vacated. The second heap is now allowed to rot down, and fresh material is put where the first heap was. How much fresh material you are creating will dictate how large the heaps are.

When you are turning your compost, aim to invert and mix up all the material. A garden fork or pitchfork is easier than a spade. Turning monthly is adequate to aerate the heap, but the more often you turn it, the faster it will turn into a useable compost. With regular turning, you should have something you can dig into your beds in six months to a year.

Covering your heap, with old carpet (not impregnated with chemicals or artificial fibres), hessian sacking or heavy-duty plastic, can help to keep the heat in, and weed seeds out. If you use impermeable material, make sure the heap is not drying out too much; it needs to be moist but not wet to break down efficiently. Water it if needs be.

Once your heap is completely broken down, it should look more or less like soil. It should be dark brown, crumbly, and, if it smells at all, smell sweet. A nasty smell indicates that it rotted without enough oxygen, which can be from lack of turning, or too much green material (especially grass cuttings). If this happens, turn it again a couple of times, mixing it up and, if possible, spreading it over a larger area. Exposure to the air should remove the problem.

Using your compost

Your compost is now ready to dig in, or to be spread as mulch. To use it as a potting compost, sieve first to remove larger bits that haven't quite broken down.

Bottom line

A good compost heap is moist, warm, and aerated. Balance green and brown materials and turn regularly.

SAVING SEED TO EAT OR TO SOW NEXT YEAR

You can save the seeds from your plants to sow next year, or to eat (e.g. coriander, fennel, nigella). Saving to sow is best with annual plants, as perennials, shrubs and bulbs will take years to get to a decent size. If you are collecting seed from your cut flower modules, pick the cut flowers you want until mid- to late August and then leave the plant alone to develop seedheads. Seeds from the herb/edible flower modules will also be ready in summer – observe individual plants to see when they're ready.

Seeds need to be left on the plant until they are mature – usually when they turn brown and papery – but you need to catch them before they drop or are blown off. If you pick them when they are green the seeds haven't finished growing and won't produce new plants. Observing your plants carefully should mean you are able to harvest them successfully.

If you are not sure when the seeds are maturing, you can put a paper bag (plastic ones keep in humidity and the seeds can rot) over the seedhead, tying it up around the stem with soft string. This is most efficacious with large seedheads that are naturally wind-dispersed, such as fennel. The seedhead will dry within the bag but any falling seeds are caught. Once they are ready, cut off the stem and put the whole thing somewhere dry. Hang it up if it's in a shed to prevent the seeds being discovered and eaten by mice. After a few weeks give the bag a shake; all the seeds should be out of the seedpods by now.

Separate the seeds from the seedheads and chaff, and put them in air-tight containers for use in the kitchen. If you are collecting the seeds to sow, put each variety in a small envelope. Store in a tin or plastic box in a cool, dry place until it's time to sow them in spring. Remember to label the envelope with the name of the plant and the year you collected the seed.

GLOSSARY

3Ds and 4Ds: shorthand for the pruning basics. Before any other pruning, always remove the Dead, Dying and Diseased branches. Occasionally a fourth 'D', Duplicate, is added, to cover the removal of crossing branches.

9cm POT, POT SIZES: 9cm denotes the diameter of the top of the pot; this is the standard small pot. Larger pots are classified by their litre (l) content: 1l, 1.5l, 2l, etc.

AGM: Award of Garden Merit given by the RHS (Royal Horticultural Society), conferring excellent performance in a garden setting as a result of extensive trials.

ANAEROBICALLY: (re: the rotting process) breaking down without oxygen, resulting in the production of noxious gases and sludgy compost.

ANNUAL: a plant that germinates, grows, flowers, sets seed and dies within a year.

APHID: a sap-sucking pest. Many species, also known as greenfly and blackfly.

AXIL: the joint between the base of the leaf and the stem (or the stem and another stem), from where another shoot may grow.

BARE ROOT: plants such as fruit trees and roses can be sold bare root during the winter. They are supplied not in a pot or any compost and should be planted as soon as possible.

BASE DRESSING: an application of granular, usually controlled-release, fertiliser to bare soil before planting.

BIENNIAL: a plant that germinates and grows foliage in one year, then flowers, sets seed and dies the following year.

BIODIVERSE/ITY: The variety of different species of flora and fauna within a particular area – the more species, the more biodiverse the area is. The greater the biodiversity, the better it is for the area.

BOLT: to set seed prematurely, usually of leafy crops, making the plant taste bitter.

BOTANICAL LATIN PLANT NAMES: the standard, universal names of plants use botanical Latin, as common names vary too much.

BULB: a plant whose perennial roots form a bulb. Its flowers and foliage die back every year.

BUSH (TOMATO): some tomato plants grow as upright cordons, others as a shorter, multi-stemmed bush.

CCA: cut-and-come-again. A term applied to crops, usually salad leaves or cut flowers, that once picked will continue to grow for one or two subsequent harvests.

CHELSEA CHOP: the cutting back of late-flowering herbaceous perennials (e.g. Michaelmas daisies) by a third or half for shorter, sturdier growth and even later flowers. Done in late May, at the time of the Chelsea Flower Show.

CLIMBER: a plant that uses twining stems or tendrils to grow up canes or other supports.

COMPOST: the result of leaving dead/unwanted plant material to rot down into a nutrient-rich, soil-like substance. Produce your own with a heap in the garden or buy in bags from garden centres.

COPPICE: the pruning of fast-growing shrubs/trees such as hazel and dogwood to a low stump, either to promote the attractive young stems, to use the stems (e.g. as bean poles) or to restrict the shrub's size.

CORDON: a plant (e.g. fruit tree, tomato) trained into an upright, columnar form.

CROWN: (rhubarb/asparagus) the name given to the perennial clump of roots that form the plant; (strawberry) the base of the plant where all the stems join.

DEADHEAD: to remove flowers that have died and/or seedheads from a plant to encourage it to produce more flowers.

DRILL: a shallow trench into which seeds are sprinkled; a means of quickly sowing a thin line of seeds, as opposed to station sowing.

EPHEMERAL: a plant that germinates, flowers, sets seed and dies in less than a year, resulting in many generations growing within a year.

ESTABLISH: a plant is established when its roots are growing into the soil it has been planted into and it is able to take up water/nutrients from that soil. A plant could be established in a pot but then planted into the ground, where it would then need to establish before it was able to take up water from more than just the compost in its potted rootball.

FERTILISER: any form of nutrient supplement. Liquid forms release nutrients faster than granular. Controlled-release granular forms supply nutrients slowly over a season.

FORCING: the process of making a plant produce its fruit/vegetable earlier than it would otherwise by adding protection and/or altering the conditions around it.

GONE OVER: when a flower fades or an annual plant dies at the end of the season.

HARDEN(ING) OFF: The process of acclimatising young plants grown in a greenhouse or other protective structure to the outdoor temperature before planting into the soil.

HERBACEOUS PERENNIAL: a plant that has topgrowth that grows, flowers and dies back every year, but roots that live all year round.

HERBICIDE: a chemical that will kill all plants, usually a spray such as 'Roundup'.

HULL: the green leafy part that joins the top of a strawberry or raspberry to the stem.

LEACH: the draining of water-soluble nutrients through the soil beyond the reach of the plants' roots.

LOAM: the ideal soil type, a mix of clay, sand and silt particles with a good proportion of organic matter and beneficial soil organisms. Easy to dig and fertile.

MICROCLIMATE: a collection of weather conditions specific to a small space.

MILDEW: a fungal disease of plants, affecting leaves and flowers.

MODULE TRAY: a rectangular plastic tray divided into 10–100 individual cells in which to grow small plug plants.

MULCH: a layer of organic matter over the soil to suppress weeds and retain soil moisture.

MYCORRHIZAL FUNGI: beneficial fungi that can be applied to plant roots to aid establishment and growth. By growing into the roots and the soil, the fungi dramatically expand the surface area of the roots for taking up water and nutrients.

NITROGEN: a plant nutrient used for growth. Deficiency shows as yellowing leaves.

ORGANIC MATTER: a catch-all term for any compost or manure that you might add to your soil to improve it, including garden compost, well-rotted horse manure, council green waste compost, leaf mould or bags from the garden centre. It does not have to be organic, i.e. free from chemicals, to be organic matter.

PERENNIAL: any plant that grows year-on-year. May be herbaceous or evergreen.

pH: the measure of acidity/alkalinity of the soil, on a scale of 1 to 14, with 1 being the most acidic and 14 the most alkaline. Most soils are between pH5 and pH8, and the ideal for most plants is pH6.5–7.

PHOSPHORUS: a plant nutrient needed for strong root growth.

PHOTOSYNTHESIS: the process by which plants make their own food using energy from the sun.

PIP: a small corm (type of bulb), typically of anemones.

PLUG PLANT: a small plant grown in a module tray ready to pot on or plant out. The rootball is consequently plug-shaped. Many retailers sell annual plants this way.

POLLINATION GROUP: a means of classifying fruit trees by the time of year they flower. Trees must be planted with others in the same or adjacent groups to ensure good pollination.

POTASSIUM: a plant nutrient needed for good flowering and fruiting. Its official chemical name is kalium, hence the 'K' for its symbol.

POT ON: to plant a small potted plant into a bigger pot to allow it to grow more (before planting into the soil).

POTTED: a plant that has been grown, and is being sold, in a pot.

PROPAGATE: to create plants by sowing seeds or taking cuttings.

PROPAGATOR (heated): a covered tray, sometimes with an electrically heated base, in which to raise seeds and small plants.

RHIZOME: a plant root. Creeping rhizomes, typically of weeds, grow out into the soil in long strands from which new shoots are generated.

ROOTBALL: the whole of the roots of a plant. Usually applied to potted plants, in which case it also refers to the soil/compost within that rootball, i.e. everything that doesn't fall off when it is lifted out of the pot.

ROOTBOUND: when a plant has been grown in a pot for too long and its roots are encircling its own rootball.

ROOT FLARE: the point at which the single stem/trunk of a tree or shrub divides into multiple roots.

ROOT PLATE: the flat area on the base of garlic cloves, onion sets and bulbs from which new roots will grow when they are planted.

ROOTSTOCK: fruit trees are generally not grown on their own roots but on a root system of another tree that has particular qualities. A branch or bud of the fruit variety is grafted (physically attached) to a young rootstock tree. The rootstock tree is not allowed to develop branches, so that the topgrowth and fruit is all of the fruit variety, and the roots are all of the rootstock. Rootstocks can confer vigour, or lack of vigour, to the variety tree, so the gardener can select a tree on a rootstock that will keep a tree small or make it big.

RUNNER: a horizontal stem put out by a plant (e.g. strawberries) on which miniature plants form, ready to root when they touch the ground.

SEASON, THE: (or, the growing season) refers to the time from spring to autumn when most vegetable- and flower-growing is completed.

SEED LEAVES: the first leaf or pair of leaves a seed pushes out of the soil.

SELF-FERTILE: a plant that doesn't need another for pollination.

SET (ONION): small onions that are planted to grow into larger onions for harvesting; a speedier process than sowing onion seed.

SHRUB: an evergreen or deciduous plant with woody stems that do not die back in winter.

SPECIES: a type of plant that differs from others but still retains certain characteristics of the group, e.g. *Rosmarinus officinalis* is the usual rosemary; *Rosmarinus prostratus* has a prostrate (i.e. horizontal along the ground) growth habit, but is still a rosemary.

STATION SOW: The sowing of seeds in the soil in individual holes a designated width apart (as opposed to sowing in a drill).

STEPOVER: a style of growing fruit trees where the main stem/trunk is trained up a short distance then along a horizontal wire. Usually grown as edging for another bed, low enough to step over.

STOLON: a stem, such as a strawberry runner, that grows parallel with the ground and can produce new plants where it touches the soil.

SUBSOIL: the layer of soil beneath the topsoil; it has fewer nutrients and a lower organic matter content.

TOP DRESSING: applying granular fertiliser to the soil after planting, around the base of the plants.

TOPGROWTH: all above-ground parts of the plant.

TOPSOIL: the layer of soil visible without digging, it contains the most nutrients and organic matter. It varies in depth across the country and even within gardens.

TREE: a single-stemmed plant whose woody topgrowth does not die back in winter.

TRUE LEAVES: the first leaf or pair of leaves that the seedling grows after the seed leaves; they will be characteristic of the plant's usual leaf shape.

TRUSS: a group of fruits on a single stem off a plant, typically tomatoes.

TURVE: a piece of turf/lawn with grass and its roots in a shallow layer of soil, typically sold in rectangular strips of $1m^2$, but also applying to strips cut out and removed from a lawn.

VARIETIES: most plants have several varieties of the species, which have been discovered or bred. Their differences are less than those between species, e.g. only in flower colour. For ease of reference in this book, the botanical 'cultivar' and 'variety' are both referred to as varieties.

DIGGING for VICTORY

THE BOOK OF HERBS

T GUIDE to the EDIBLE GARDEN   Joe Hashman

Joy Lar

Grow your own Vegeta

Forgotten Fruits   C

EGETABLE & FRUIT GARD

The Medicine Garden

Science and the Garden   INGRAM, VINCE-

KA McVICAR   JEKKA'S COMPLETE   herb b

W BIGGS'S COMPLETE
VEGETABLES (REVISED EDITION)

PESTS AND DIS

FURTHER READING

This book has all you need to get started on growing your own food and flowers, but you may want to find out more detail. Seed packets and the internet are a great, free, place to start, but other books are also recommended below.

Websites
www.hollyefarrell.com
The author's website. Blogs on garden projects, recipes and homemaking. Contact the author through the site.

http://www.rhs.org.uk
The website of the Royal Horticultural Society. Extensive resources include advice on general growing your own; pests and diseases and (fruit) pruning; plant selector tool; information on plants for pollinators; and much more.

http://www.gardenorganic.org.uk
The website of Garden Organic, a charity promoting organic growing. Advice and information on growing your own and organic best practice; online catalogue of seeds, plants and garden supplies; the home of the Heritage Seed Library (members can have a limited number of seed varieties per year). Suppliers of comfrey 'Bocking 14' plants.

Books
Vegetable and Fruit Gardening (2012) The Royal Horticultural Society. Dorling Kindersley.
Grow Your Own Vegetables (2002) Joy Larkcom. Frances Lincoln.
Jekka's Complete Herb Book (2009) Jekka McVicar. Kyle Cathie.
Grow Your Own Cut Flowers (2002) Sarah Raven. BBC Books.
The Royal Horticultural Society Pests and Diseases (2009) Andrew Halstead and Pippa Greenwood. Dorling Kindersley.
Science and the Garden: The Scientific Basis of Horticultural Practice (2008) D.S. Ingram, D. Vince-Prue and P.J. Gregory. Wiley-Blackwell.
Organic Gardening: The Natural No-dig Way (2010) Charles Dowding. Green Books.
What Will I Do With All Those Courgettes? (2002) Elaine Borish. Fidelio Press.

Sources of heritage and heirloom seeds
Heritage Seed Library (http://www.gardenorganic.org.uk/hsl/).
Pennard Plants (http://www.pennardplants.com).
Some of the larger seed merchants also offer a limited selection of heirloom varieties.

INDEX

PLANTS AND PLANTING PLANS FOR A BEE GARDEN
How to design beautiful borders that will attract bees

MAUREEN LITTLE

This book will enable you to select bee-friendly plants, and to plan borders which are beneficial to bees, encouraging these most valuable of insects to come to your garden over and over again, both for sustenance and to aid pollination. It contains a wide range of practical, beautiful and easy-to-follow planting plans for bee-friendly gardens of all sizes, including: traditional mixed, cottage- and colour-themed borders; 'designer' and 'natural' borders; borders for acid and alkaline soils; ideas for container planting. It also includes over 180 colour illustrations.

£14.99   978-1-905862-80-1

THE KITCHEN HERB GARDEN
A seasonal guide to growing, cooking and using culinary herbs

MAUREEN LITTLE

This illustrated book will enable you to enjoy cultivating a kitchen herb garden and using its fresh home-grown herbs in your cooking. There is detailed information on how to plan, plant, grow and maintain thirty selected herbs, together with over sixty delicious recipes – from soups to sauces – for using herbs in your kitchen. You'll also find information on:

• *Using herbs to flavour oils, vinegars, butters, sugars and jellies*

• *How to harvest, dry and preserve your herbs*

• *How to grow herbs in containers*

• *How to match herbs to ingredients in your cooking*

£14.99   978-1-905862-89-4